Comparative
Industrial Relations

Comparative Industrial Relations

Contemporary Research and Theory

edited by

Roy J. Adams

HarperCollins*Academic*
An imprint of HarperCollins*Publishers*

Published by
HarperCollinsAcademic
77–85 Fulham Palace Road
Hammersmith
London W6 8JB
UK

First published in 1991

British Library Cataloguing in Publication Data

Comparative industrial relations : contemporary research and theory.
1.   Industrial relations
I.   Adams, Roy J.
331

ISBN 0–04–445966–1
ISBN 0–04–445967–X pbk

Library of Congress Cataloging in Publication Data

Comparative industrial relations : contemporary research and theory /
edited by Roy J. Adams.
    p.   cm.
Includes bibliographical references and index.
ISBN 0–04–445966–1 (HB) : $44.95 –
ISBN 0–04–445967–X (PB) : $17.95
1. Industrial relations. 2. Comparative management. I. Adams, Roy J.
HD6971.C72   1991
331—dc20   90–43868
                                                        CIP

Typset 10 on 12 point Garamond
Printed in Great Britain by
Billing & Sons Ltd, Worcester

Contents

Contributors

ROY J. ADAMS
Professor of Industrial Relations, McMaster University and 1990–1 Canadian Pacific Distinguished Visiting Professor of Industrial Relations, University of Toronto, Canada

JACK BARBASH
Professor of Economics and Industrial Relations (Emeritus), University of Wisconsin–Madison and Visiting Professor, Graduate School of Management, University of California, Davis, California

TAYO FASHOYIN
Professor of Labour and Industrial Relations, University of Lagos, Nigeria and 1989–90 Fulbright Scholar, The Wharton School, University of Pennsylvania, United States

LAJOS HÉTHY
Director, Institute of Labour Research, Budapest, Hungary and Deputy Secretary of State, Hungarian Ministry of Labour

BERNDT K. KELLER
Professor of Political Science, University of Constance, Federal Republic of Germany

NOAH M. MELTZ
Professor of Economics and Industrial Relations, University of Toronto, Canada

DAVID PLOWMAN
Professor of Industrial Relations and Head, School of Industrial Relations and Organizational Behaviour, University of New South Wales, Australia

ROBERT PRICE
Head, Policy Co–ordination and International Affairs Division, Economic and Social Research Council, United Kingdom

MARK THOMPSON
William M. Hamilton Professor of Industrial Relations, University of British Columbia, Canada

Preface

Early in 1988 I was asked to organize a session on Recent Trends in Industrial Relations Studies and Theory for the Eighth World Congress of the International Industrial Relations Association (IIRA) which was to be held in Brussels, Belgium in September 1989. Given that charge, I contacted several outstanding scholars from universities around the world and asked them to prepare essays on aspects of industrial relations which would, in total, provide a broad-ranging review of the current state of the art in comparative industrial relations. This volume is the end result. I am grateful to Roger Blanpain, past president of the IIRA, for providing me with the opportunity to orchestrate this project and to Alan Gladstone, IIRA secretary, for his encouragement and support. Thanks are also due to Ukandi Damachi, University of Lagos, who acted as chairman at the Brussels Congress and to Chris Leggett, University of Stirling, Scotland and City Polytechnic of Hong Kong, Mick Marchington, Manchester School of Management, England, Norman Dufty, Western Australia Labour Market Research Centre, and Tony Giles, University of New Brunswick (Canada), who co-ordinated discussion and provided useful comments on the papers when they were first presented in Brussels.

Roy J. Adams
Hamilton, Canada
October, 1990

1 *Introduction and overview*

ROY J. ADAMS

Industrial relations is a very young discipline. Whereas the parent fields from which it derives – economics, law, sociology and psychology – are all well over a century old industrial relations is largely a post Second World War development.

In the 1960s, industrial relations (IR) was a concept that was practically unknown outside the Anglo-Saxon world. The creation of the International Industrial Relations Association (IIRA) in 1967, however, helped to make it a worldwide phenomenon. Today the field of IR, although still small in contrast to some of the other social sciences, has adherents on every continent.

As one of the youngest of the social sciences, the approach of industrial relations to the empirical world is still in a state of flux. Among the most important and well-known efforts to date to provide a general framework capable of guiding research and theory on a global basis was the formalization by John Dunlop of the conception of industrial relations system (IRS). The chapter by Noah Meltz in this volume reviews its status today, three decades after it was first proposed. He notes that Dunlop developed the model in order 'to provide tools of analysis to interpret and to gain understanding of the widest possible range of industrial relations facts and practices'. The model was composed of actors (labour, management, and the state) each with its own ideology and power interacting to produce outcomes, which Dunlop called 'rules', within a context of technological, market and power constraints.

This model has been criticized for being static rather than dynamic; for implicitly valuing stability over social change; for positing a shared ideology between labour and management; for ignoring many behavioural aspects of the employment relationship; for failing to employ testable hypotheses; and for its focus on rules rather than on the broader expanse of phenomena addressed by industrial relations researchers. After carefully reviewing Dunlop's book, and, indeed, interviewing Professor Dunlop, Meltz rejects most of these criticisms.

Dunlop did not intend the concept 'rules' to be interpreted literally but rather he meant it to refer to a wide range of IR outcomes from wages to bargaining arrangements; he specifically stated his hope that researchers would use the model to investigate how systems change over time. He did indicate his belief that a shared ideology would be the norm, but Meltz argues that Dunlop in fact anticipated breakdowns in those understandings. Moreover, contrary to the assertions of some critics, Meltz does find hypotheses implicit in Dunlopian theory. For example, Dunlop predicted that in systems in which there is little ideological consensus there would be turbulence and instability.

If Meltz is right why have the critics been so wrong? I believe that they have erred because they have considered Dunlop's model to be either a subset of Talcott Parsons's conception of a social system or a specific manifestation of general systems theory. Dunlop, however, does not seem to have intended that it be considered a version of either of those schemes. Instead, even though he made reference to Parsons's work, he seems to have wanted IRS to be regarded as an independent formalization of those persistent patterns of labour, management and state interaction that we see about us every day. Certainly that is how the framework generally has been used. Today it is widely embraced around the world as a device for organizing industrial relations courses and textbooks (see Adams 1990). Its major failure, however, has been its inability to stimulate hypothesis-testing research. It has, Meltz tells us, encouraged relatively few studies of this sort.

Although the IR systems framework has not been unanimously acclaimed it has, nevertheless, provided the linchpin necessary to hold together a worldwide community of scholars in pursuit of knowledge about employment relations. In general that community is concerned less with the abstract conceptual riddles that take up so much of the energy of economic and social theorists than it is with practical solutions to practical problems (Adams 1988). In his chapter on John R. Commons, Jack Barbash provides a portrait of the quintessential industrial relationist. As Barbash sees it, J. R. Commons was one of the founders of the Western industrial relations tradition. Co-founders were Sidney and Beatrice Webb, Karl Marx, Frederick Taylor and Elton Mayo. Each of them placed labour at the centre of a body of intellectual ideas in contrast to the conventional economists' dehumanization and marginalization of labour.

Commons's particular contribution was twofold. He developed a body of theory and, perhaps even more important, he created a method or style. He argued that the relationship between labour and management was fundamentally unequal in the modern employment situation. He believed that state of affairs to be morally unacceptable in a democratic society and thus defined the central problem of industrial relations as being the pursuit not only of economic efficiency but also of equity, justice, and the liberation of human potential. He argued that unions and collective bargaining were essential pillars of any democratic society. Collective agreements, he taught us, should be seen not simply as economic transactions but rather as 'constitutions for industrial government'.

His method was that of the participant-investigator. In addition to being a researcher and teacher, he was also a mediator, administrator, negotiator and drafter of legislation. He spent as much time in the real world as he did in the ivory tower. He wanted radically to improve labour welfare but in contrast to Marx he proposed to do it by the conservative means of collective bargaining, legislation, and employer enlightenment.

Commons is not widely known outside the United States, Barbash tells us, but, it seems to me, his spirit is nevertheless evident throughout the worldwide community of industrial relations scholars. Among the traits that tend to distinguish industrial relations everywhere from other social science disciplines is a greater concern with and engagement in practical policy matters and a search for solutions to labour problems which provide for a balance of efficiency and equity.

Because of its roots in the Anglo-Saxon world the conceptual apparatus of industrial relations finds its best 'fit' in the industrialized market economy countries. Indeed, as Lajos Héthy states, until recently in Eastern Europe industrial relations as a theoretical construct was generally unknown and if known it was unacceptable because of its implication that employers and employees have separate interests which produce conflicts in need of resolution through mechanisms such as collective bargaining.

In the 1980s, however, IR concepts became more applicable as enterprise managers were given more flexibility within rational economic planning frameworks to develop unique strategies at the firm level. In some countries 'diverging and conflicting interests' among workers, enterprise managers and state agencies were being recognized and mechanisms for the resolution of conflict were being developed. Trade unions, enterprises and the state began to take on distinctive roles. As a result, the extreme unitarist frame of reference (to generalize Alan Fox's term) within which not only management and labour but also the state are deemed to have a singular outlook and set of interests became less relevant and less viable as a tool of analysis (Fox 1966). Enterprise managers were no longer simply state bureaucrats and trade unions could no longer be classified as mere 'transmission belts'.

In the fall of 1989 several communist regimes were replaced altogether in Eastern Europe and the second world system of industrial relations began rapidly to collapse. By mid-1990 industrial relations were in a state of flux as new institutions, such as trade unions independent of the state, appeared and old ones vanished.

The emergence of pluralism in Eastern Europe must be met with keen interest in the West. As new solutions are developed to old problems many lessons (some perhaps generalizable to other parts of the world) are to be learned.

Concepts developed with Western institutions in mind also fit less well in the developing countries with their large agricultural populations, extreme poverty, and marginal labour force participants (International Labour Office 1987). Nevertheless, we do find institutions such as trade unions, employer organizations and collective bargaining in most developing countries. By far, however, it is the state, Tayo Fashoyin tells us, that is the dominant actor in most of these countries. It is the state that generally takes prime responsibility for leading the development effort. Trade unions and collective bargaining are tolerated but closely controlled. Unlike the West where the primary focus of research has been on the labour–management relationship, the dominant role of the state in the developing countries has led to a focus on union–state relations. Thus, while a good deal is known about relations between labour and government in many developing countries, less is known about labour–management relations. Collective bargaining, especially at the level of the firm, is under-studied. Initiatives in a few countries regarding workers' participation have produced some research which indicates an unfortunate general failure of these procedures to perform up to expectations. Apart from labour relations a good deal of research has been carried out in developing countries on labour markets. Employment, training, mobility, labour force attachment, and wages have all been the focuses of research, much of it sponsored by the International Labour Office as part of its World Employment Programme.

The predominance of IR research on developing countries, Fashoyin tells us, is now being carried out by resident nationals rather than by researchers from the Western industrialized countries. In the 1950s and 1960s – the era when so many countries in Africa and Asia were winning their independence – interest in the West was keen. As the romance of the struggle for independence has faded, however, so apparently has Western interest.

In the industrialized market countries the past decade has seen a major sea-change. The 1970s was an era of rapidly rising prices, high levels of industrial conflict, and initiatives by governments to bring labour organizations into the policy-making process (see e.g. Juris *et al.* 1985). It was a time of expanding labour rights both collective and individual. Labour organizations were the dominant initiators of change and employers were on the defensive. After a deep recession cum depression in the early 1980s, however, these trends generally came to a halt. Unemployment rose to levels reminiscent of the 1930s and labour's power dissipated. Management seized the initiative in many countries to change IR practices previously well established.

Governments also were active initiators of change. Instead of responding to the pleas of labour for more security, equality, participation, and entitlements, generally governments answered positively management demands for less regulation and more 'flexibility' in pursuit of international competitiveness. Japan emerged as a serious challenger to Western economic dominance. Since Japanese industrial relations practices were given credit by many observers for a good part of Japanese economic success, they were widely studied and, in modified form, increasingly emulated by Western firms.

These changes led to new developments in research and theory. In his chapter David Plowman demonstrates that management as an actor in IR systems was given much closer attention than previously it had been. US theorists Kochan, Katz and McKersie drew on the work of Chandler to emphasize the importance of the concept of strategic choice in understanding the functioning of IR systems (Kochan *et al.* 1984). At any point in time, they argued, the actors in IR systems may choose to continue operating within accepted parameters or may seek to change those parameters. In the United States during the 1970s and 1980s it became increasingly clear that managers of key corporations were trying to change fundamentally the nature of the American system. Not only were they insisting that labour accept drastically different conditions of work but many of them were actively trying to destroy the labour movement (Adams 1989). This extreme behaviour does not seem to have been followed vigorously in any of the other industrialized, market economy countries (IMECs). Nevertheless, managers throughout the IMEC countries have sought, as Mark Thompson tells us, more decentralized bargaining and more flexibility. In particular, the Japanese practices of multi–skilling, flexible work assignment, worker participation in productivity enhancement exercises, and income based to some extent on firm performance were ideas which became increasingly attractive to Western management. Should such practices become prevalent – as some observers believe to be likely – the result would be IR systems radically different from those in existence during the 1960s and 1970s.

Another stream of management research has focused largely on the methods used by management to extract usable work from the labour force. This stream has developed the useful concepts of frontier of control and labour process which have allowed us to see aspects of the employment relationship in new and fresh ways. This literature, which Plowman briefly reviews, is growing rapidly.

Recent research on trade unions has focused largely on the decline of union power and membership during the 1980s.[1] In several countries (the United States, France, the United Kingdom, the Netherlands) union membership has decreased very substantially in the 1980s; in others there has been decline but it has been less precipitous (e.g. Italy, West Germany, Japan). In still others (Sweden, Denmark) it has increased. Moreover, in some countries, (Sweden, Denmark, Belgium) union membership as a percentage of the labour force is very high, while in others (France and the United States) it is very low. This variation between countries at a similar stage of economic development presents a great challenge to the IR theorist. Price in his chapter responds to that challenge. He argues (consistent with John Dunlop it may be noted) that within IR systems, at most times, there exist certain institutional arrangements and an at least implicit 'accord' (might one not call it a shared ideology?) between actors to honour those arrangements. During such periods econometric models often are effective in explaining patterns of union growth and decline. However, a model developed in country A will not necessarily be effective in country B because of differences in institutional arrangements. Thus an increase in unemployment is widely associated with decreasing membership but in those countries where unions have some responsibility for unemployment insurance benefits (e.g. Belgium, Sweden) union membership is likely to increase.

At certain critical times, Price tells us, there will be 'paradigm breaks'. The old accord will collapse leading to a crisis. Notable examples include the United States in the 1930s, Germany after the First World War and Britain in the 1890s (and possibly the United States currently). What accounts for the advent and resolution of these periods of change? Price suggests that crises may be precipitated by a wide range of factors – including economic ones – but that their resolution 'will be decided by the interplay of the collective power of organizations, classes and ruling groups rather than by purely economic processes'.

It was certain, on entering the 1980s, that trade unions were permanent institutions in all of the countries of the liberal-democratic world. Having left the 1980s that proposition is no longer so clear. For theory and practice the implications of the alternative are enormous.

The state, as Berndt Keller notes, has received less attention (in the IMEC countries at least) than have the other actors. We lack research and theory on such questions as: why does one state choose to intervene in the system to a much greater extent than another (e.g. West Germany vs the United Kingdom) and to what result? Does a great deal of intervention and 'juridification' result in rigidities which in turn make it more difficult for management to do what is prudent in order to compete internationally? The experience of countries such as Sweden and West Germany as well as more general research by Korpi (1985) on the relationship between productivity and the extent of welfare state provisions and by Freeman & Medoff (1984) on the relationship between productivity and collective bargaining in the United States seem to suggest the opposite. The relationship between productivity and regulation is certainly not a simple one. It will require a good deal more research in order to unravel the complex contingencies which lead to high vs low productivity performance.

Also being asked by theorists is the question as to why there is more state intervention in some periods than in others. One form of state intervention – generally labelled neo-corporatism – has drawn considerable attention during the past two decades. Apparently, when the market power of the labour movement is very high and that power is seen to be the cause of economic problems (e.g. wage-push inflation) the state (in nations with strong liberal democratic traditions at least) will try to co-opt it, or in the current terminology it will try to 'incorporate' it (Panitch 1977). Where labour is not seen to have much power the state (especially if controlled by a conservative party) will largely ignore it or, as in Britain and the United States, will follow policies apparently designed to ensure that it never again becomes 'a problem'. Certainly, governments friendly to labour may use this technique continually regardless of economic and social conditions. Neo-corporatism may be considered one of a range of strategic policy choices open to governments.

Additional research on this topic has sought to identify the conditions under which neo-corporatism is likely to be successfully utilized. The experience of the 1970s and 1980s has provided a storehouse of data from which empirical generalization is now being wrested.

Research in industrial relations has long 'followed the headlines', to use Milton Derber's phrase (Derber 1967), and that tradition continues today. Thompson notes, for example, that as the focus of industrial relations decision-making has become more decentralized, plant level studies have become more fashionable, especially in the United States, after a decade or more of predominantly macro-statistical research. In the intensely competitive atmosphere of the 1980s productivity has become the most prevalent dependent variable in IR research in contrast to the 1970s when researchers focused more on the issues of equity and democracy.

The chapters included in this volume as well as the workshop discussions which followed their original presentation at the Eighth World Congress of the International Industrial Relations Association suggest that industrial relations as a field of inquiry has a definite character which distinguishes it from the other social sciences. Among the defining characteristics of industrial relations as a field of inquiry are the following. First, industrial relationists have the ambition of understanding the employment relationship in its totality in contrast to the limited aspects of labour–management–state relations addressed by other branches of the social sciences. Second, industrial relations researchers have continually demonstrated a normative concern not only with economic efficiency but also with equity, justice, and democracy. Finally, industrial relationists tend to be more concerned with finding practical solutions to contemporary problems than with building elegant but esoteric conceptual structures. Thus theory in IR is not so well developed as it is in other branches of social science. Nevertheless, IR theory as a conscious focus of intellectual endeavour has been expanding during the 1980s.

Industrial relationists are beginning to realize that theory is not simply a synonym for the impractical. It is a shorthand for what we know above and beyond specific events occurring in specific places at specific times. Theory is pervasive and the challenge is to make it public and explicit, to refine it, to test it and gradually to produce deeper understanding and enduring generalizations. The chapters that follow provide the field with a sort of baseline against which future progress may be assessed.

Notes

1 See the papers prepared for a symposium on the future of trade unionism published in *Labour and Society* **13**, 2 April 1988.

References

Adams, R. J. 1988. Desperately seeking industrial relations theory. *International Journal of Comparative Labour Law and Industrial Relations* **4**, 1, Spring, 1–10.

Adams, R. J. 1989. North American industrial relations: divergent trends in Canada and the United States. *International Labour Review* **128**, 1, 47–64.

Adams, R. J. 1990. Teaching comparative industrial relations: results of an informal multinational survey. Paper presented at the annual meeting of the Canadian Industrial Relations Association, Victoria, British Columbia, 4 June.

Derber, Milton 1967. *Research on Labor Problems in the United States*. New York: Random House.

Fox, A. 1966. *Industrial Sociology and Industrial Relations*. London: HMSO.

Freeman R. B. & J. L. Medoff 1984. *What Do Unions Do?* New York: Basic Books.

International Labour Office 1987. *World Labour Report–3*. Oxford: Oxford University Press.

Juris, H., M. Thompson & W. Daniels (eds) 1985. *Industrial Relations in a Decade of Economic Change*. Madison, Wisc.: Industrial Relations Research Association.

Kochan, T. A., R. B. McKersie & P. Capelli 1984. Strategic choice and industrial relations theory. *Industrial Relations* **23**, 1, Winter, 16–39.

Korpi, Walter 1985. Economic growth and the welfare system: leaky bucket or irrigation system? *European Sociological Review* **1**, 2 September, 97–118.

Panitch, L. 1977. The development of corporatism in liberal democracies. *Comparative Political Studies* **10**, 61–90.

2 *Dunlop's* Industrial Relations Systems *after three decades*

NOAH M. MELTZ

Dunlop's superb thought-piece *Industrial Relations Systems*, published in 1958, has been perhaps the most influential book in the field of industrial relations since the Second World War. The purpose of this chapter is to consider the impact on the field of industrial relations of Dunlop's book, which for shorthand purposes I will designate as *IRS*.[1] The impact will be considered from two perspectives: the extent to which current theories and frameworks of IR draw on *IRS*; and second, the degree to which Dunlop succeeded in the task he set for *IRS*, 'to provide tools of analysis to interpret and to gain understanding of the widest possible range of industrial relations facts and practices' (p. vii).

This chapter is not intended as a review of the extensive writings or other substantial contributions of Professor Dunlop. The focus is solely on *Industrial Relations Systems*. The chapter is also not a review of the voluminous literature describing, commenting on, criticizing, supporting, amending or applying *IRS*.[2] That is a separate task.

The chapter begins with an overview of *IRS* focusing in particular on what Dunlop indicated was needed as a theoretical framework for industrial relations and what he set out as a model to meet the needs. Second, I will briefly indicate the kinds of criticisms which were directed at *IRS* as well as its usefulness through attempts to apply it – the ultimate test of a successful theory according to Dunlop. Third, as a proxy measure for the book's role in the field, I indicate the extent to which Dunlop's *IRS* is cited. Fourth, I consider the links between *IRS* and the theoretical framework developed by Kochan, Katz & McKersie in their widely cited study *The Transformation of*

American Industrial Relations (1986). Finally, I consider the extent to which the task Dunlop set out to achieve has been met.

The objectives and basic model of *IRS*

The following statement by Dunlop summarizes the main objective of *IRS* (p. 6):

> An industrial relations system is logically an abstraction ... [not] concerned with behaviour as a whole. There are no actors whose whole activity is confined *solely* to the industrial relations ... sphere(s), although some may approach this limit ... an industrial relations system is [not] designed simply to describe in factual terms the real world of time and space ... [it is an] abstraction(s) designed to highlight relationships and to focus attention upon critical variables and to formulate propositions for historical inquiry and statistical testing.[3] (italics in original)

The key words are: abstraction, critical variables, formulate propositions, statistical testing. With these, the discipline of industrial relations will develop a theoretical core and research will be more additive.

Dunlop's *IRS* contains abstractions in the form of actors in the system, the contexts of the system, and the ideology of the system, which combine to establish rules to govern the actors at the work place and in the work community. The dependent variables are the rules. The critical independent variables are the contexts of the system which can change, and the ideology of the system which is the combination of the ideologies of each of the actors. The combination of ideologies may be stable or unstable.

There are three major groupings of actors: managers and their representatives; workers (non-managerial) and any spokesman; and specialized governmental agencies (and specialized private agencies) dealing with managers' or workers' organizations or even individual workers. There are, in turn, three sets of variables in the environmental context which are fundamental in determining the rules which govern the work place: the technological characteristics of the work place and work community;[4] the market or budgeting constraints which affect the actors; the location and distribution of power in the larger society.

Technological characteristics of the work place are important factors in determining the kinds of skills needed in an organization and the proportions of each. Market or budgetary factors set the limits within which the organization must operate. The location and distribution of power in society influences the extent to which the *IRS* is centralized or decentralized as well as the kinds of interventions, by whom and for what purpose.

Each of the actors has an ideology or a set of beliefs concerning its own role and place and that of the other actors in the system. While in general there tends to be a compatibility among the beliefs, there can also be a situation where there is no common ideology, where at least one actor does not provide a legitimate role for the other. While Dunlop wrote this in 1958, it is clearly relevant today. Kochan *et al.* (1986) indicate the increasing social and political acceptability for management in the United States to embrace publicly a 'union free' preference. More and more the management actor does not accept that there is a legitimate role for the union actor. Such a situation, Dunlop says, would lead to volatile relationships with no stability likely to be achieved (p. 17). This is separate from disputes over terms and conditions of employment which take place within an accepted framework. Clearly the ideologies can change with implications for both the stability of the system as well as particular outcomes (rules).

Dunlop identifies the outcome of the *IRS* as rules for resolving conflicts among the actors, and substantive rules, that is, the specific terms and conditions of employment. Unfortunately, there is a confusing use of the word 'rules' to refer to both the process of resolving disputes and the specific terms and conditions of employment such as the wage rates, hours of employment, etc.[5] Some of the criticism of Dunlop's model seems to imply that it is only concerned with the first type of rules whereas the text clearly indicates that both are part of the model (for example, see pp. 5, 19, 20, 24).

A second possible source of confusion is that an industrial relations system means different things at different levels of aggregation. For Dunlop, an *IRS* seems to be the particular mechanism by which workers (whether organized or unorganized) reach an understanding with managers on the terms and conditions of employment. The particular mechanism can change over time even in specific organizations. In addition, what is actually determined, that is, the precise outcome, will change as there are changes in one or more of the technological, market, power and status factors.

Despite the possible sources of confusion as to what Dunlop means by rules and an IR system, a distinct IR model is developed. What is to be determined are two dependent variables; the process for resolving differences over the terms and conditions of employment (general rules); and the specific terms and conditions of employment (substantive rules) in individual organizations, in industries, for an entire economy and even for a number of different countries. What determines these two dependent variables is affected by the level of aggregation under consideration. This is a three-dimensional model: actors; context; and level of aggregation. The impact of changes in the independent variables (technology, market or budget constraints, the political power of the actors and their status) is intended to be ultimately measurable.

Criticisms of IRS
There are five major criticisms of Dunlop's *Industrial Relations Systems* model. First, as noted above, it is claimed that having rules as the dependent variable is not very meaningful because it neglects the specific aspects of what has occurred in the actual negotiations between unions and management. I have already indicated that Dunlop used the word 'rules' in two different ways, as a process and as the specific details or terms and conditions of a collective agreement. Second, the model is criticized for being static. The text makes clear that changes will occur both in the processes used by labour and management and also in the substantive outcomes. In fact Dunlop is very explicit that the intent of his model is to explain why changes occur over time in the two kinds of rules (see p. 27). Third, the model is said to assume that there is a balance between labour and management through a shared ideology.[6] This criticism is also an extension of the criticism of a lack of dynamism. The text makes it clear that 'a congruence or compatibility' of views exists only in certain IR systems and only for certain periods of time (p. 17). In fact one of the objectives of the *IRS* model is to identify the determinants of a common ideology and how and why and in what direction it has changed or may change. Fourth, the model is said to ignore behavioural aspects of the labour–management relationship. It is difficult to understand the source of this criticism when Dunlop distinguishes between formal and informal rules in the work place (pp. 7–8). The primary task of the model is to determine what is

actually occurring at the work place and the role of various types of influences on the actors.

The fifth and final[7] criticism I will identify is that the model does not generate any testable hypotheses. It is said to be merely a tautology which identifies the factors which interact to determine wages and working conditions (and what Craig 1986 calls organizational outputs – union security, management rights, etc.). While this is indeed the approach which many of the adapters of Dunlop's model have followed, this does not seem to have been Dunlop's intention. *IRS* makes it clear that the objective is statistical testing (p. 6). The text also indicated the factors which can alter the *IRS*; for example, chapter 2 discusses the features of the technical context which can affect the outcomes of the *IRS*, while chapter 3 does the same for the impact of different product markets. The whole intent is to generate testable hypotheses. Did he develop testable hypotheses? Is it possible to develop such hypotheses through his model?

An examination of the application of Dunlop's model is beyond the scope of this chapter especially when consideration would also have to be given to the applications of the adaptations of IRS. Dunlop himself included in the text international comparisons of IRSs in the bituminous coal industry and building (construction). As a summary comment, it can be said that few if any of the applications conducted statistical tests of hypotheses which were generated by the model. Instead the model has served as a general framework to organize a description of the interaction between the actors, the environmental contexts and the ideologies. While the application of the model as a framework is certainly useful, it does not meet the stronger test set by Dunlop of the statistical testing of hypotheses and of making the research more additive.

The impact of IRS on other writers

While we will not trace the impact of *IRS* on industrial relations, Adams (1989) found *IRS* to be the primary framework used around the world for organizing comparative IR courses. To provide a rough measure of the impact of Dunlop's original research I have included statistics of the extent to which authors of social science articles have cited *IRS*. It is possible, of course, that a citation could simply indicate that the authors were paying pro forma reference to *IRS* without its playing any substantial role in the discussion. To consider the specific role *IRS* played would require an examination of each of the 125 articles in which *IRS* has been cited over the past 22 years.

Table 2.1 Social science citations of Dunlop's Industrial
relations systems.

Period	No. of citations	
1966–70		9
1971–5		6
1976–80		30
1981–5		48
1984	10	
1987	16	
1988	8	
1989	14	
1990 (January to April)	1	49
Total*		142

* Excludes self-citations

Source: Social sciences citation index, Institute for Scientific Information,
Philadelphia, Pa: various issues.

Instead we will simply comment on the trend which appears to have
emerged.

Table 2.1 shows the record of citations of *IRS* in social science
journals over the past 22 years. Since the book was originally
published in 1958, there are eight years for which no record of
citations has been tabulated. The table shows a slow start in citations
then a gathering of momentum which reached a peak in this decade.
In fact, the period of 1986–April 1990 has already produced the
largest count yet of citations to *IRS*.

It is not possible to say specifically that the impact of *IRS* has
been increasing over time. It is possible to say that scholars in
industrial relations are increasingly aware of Dunlop's *Industrial
Relations Systems*. Whether they agree, disagree or are neutral, one
can at least say that the awareness of *IRS* has certainly been growing
over time.

IRS and Kochan, Katz & McKersie

A major recent contribution to industrial relations theory is the volume by Kochan, Katz & McKersie (1986) entitled *The Transformation
of American Industrial Relations*. There is a close conceptual link
between this volume, which for shorthand purposes I will refer
to as KKM, and *IRS*. Ray Marshall appropriately summed up the
link with his comment on the dust jacket of the volume: this is
'an important book that stands comparison with John Dunlop's

classic *Industrial Relations Systems*, which it places in dynamic context'.

As discussed above, *IRS* was designed to be dynamic. However, the fundamental contribution of KKM is to introduce a more behavioural aspect to the basic Dunlop model in the sense of identifying the locus of different types and focuses of decision-making by levels of authority for all three actors. Dunlop made explicit that there are hierarchies of managers, workers and their spokespersons, and multiple interactions among and within these hierarchies. What he did not seem to do is to identify the differing objectives, strategies, and industrial relations activities of the various levels within the hierarchies of management, unions, and government. The KKM innovation adds to the potential set of testable hypotheses by introducing a key distinction to the decision-making framework of the *IRS* model. Thus the transformation model is perfectly consistent with Dunlop's *IRS*. Through the identification of three levels of industrial relations activities of the three actors, KKM have expanded the hierarchy dimension which was not fully explored in *IRS*.

The task of industrial relations theory

In his *Industrial Relations Systems*, Dunlop set out to provide an abstract though useful model which would supply the basis for a 'theoretical core to relate isolated facts, to point to new types of enquiries and to make research additive'. The bulk of commentators would say that *IRS* did not achieve the task that was set. While there were applications of *IRS*, they have tended to be more as a framework to describe the interrelationships of the actors in the system with each other in the context of the impact of various environmental factors. In fact *IRS* has had a profound impact on the pedagogy of IR in basic courses and in comparative IR (Adams 1989).

What then can we say about Dunlop's *IRS* after three decades? There are several observations which can be made. The first is that the volume sparked an enormous discussion within the industrial relations field. Scholars may not entirely agree with Dunlop but they cannot ignore him. Second, critics seem to have overlooked the dual focuses of his model within the concept of rule determination on both the process of establishing rules by which workers and their spokespersons, managers and their organizations, and government and private agencies set terms and conditions of employment, and on the actual terms and conditions of employment which are established in particular situations. Thus for Dunlop the purpose of the theory is to be able to examine specific developments in the work place and to test hypotheses on why they are occurring. In general, this seems not to have been done. The challenge is to apply the basic theoretical framework, modified as appropriate. Third, critics and even those sympathetic to Dunlop have suggested that he assumes a stable shared ideology and therefore that he has developed a static form of analysis. While Dunlop does suggest that a common ideology occurs, he also says that this is the product of the specific forces he identifies and that this can change over time. He explicitly states that

an industrial relations system may also be thought of as moving through time, or more rigorously, as responding to changes which affect the constitution of the system . . . changes in ideology, as a response to the larger society, may also come to have an impact on the rules established by an industrial-relations system. (p. 27)

The whole purpose of Dunlop's *IRS* is to explain the source of change. Somehow this aspect of his theory has been neglected. Fourth, while Dunlop intended the framework to provide for testable hypotheses, and in fact the volume does set out testable hypotheses, this avenue was not pursued to any great extent. Is it because of the view that there are no hypotheses to test or that the hypotheses are not testable; or that the critics in particular are not interested in developing and testing the hypotheses? Roy Adams (1988) has recently argued that there are in fact a lot of testable hypotheses. The answer seems to be that there was less interest in testing hypotheses in industrial relations. Meltz (1989) argues that this is the case because, at least in North America, there are few academic departments of industrial relations and therefore there are a limited number of scholars with incentives to advance the field (discipline) of industrial relations as opposed to contributing to other disciplines in the departments within which they are located. The original intent of *IRS* does not seem to have been fully explored. The addition of Kochan *et al.*'s three-tier levels of activity could provide a renewed incentive to explore fully whether *IRS* can provide the basis for additive research in industrial relations.

The conclusion is that after three decades, Dunlop's *Industrial Relations Systems* is alive and well and waiting to be fully applied. While the original task has not yet been fulfilled, the need for such a theoretical framework is still there. The vehicle to meet the need, even after three decades, still seems to have the best potential to provide the necessary theoretical framework, especially if Kochan *et al.*'s three levels of strategic activity are included. The task is to apply and refine the enormous contribution which Dunlop made to the field when he published *Industrial Relations Systems* in 1958.

Notes

The author would like to acknowledge the assistance received from Carolynn Alton and Bruce Pearce of the Centre for Industrial Relations, University of Toronto. Harry C. Katz and Roy Adams have provided helpful comments. A draft of the original paper was discussed with John T. Dunlop who made very useful suggestions. In the final analysis the author takes full responsibility for the observations presented in the chapter. Financial support for the research was provided by the Humanities and Social Sciences Committee of the University of Toronto.

1 American readers will associate *IRS* with the Internal Revenue Service. However, no one in industrial relations can say that Dunlop's book is taxing.

2 The following are just a few articles which refer to Dunlop's *IRS*: R. Adams, *Dunlop After Two Decades: Systems Theory as a Framework for Organizing the Field of Industrial Relations*, McMaster University, Faculty of Business, Working Paper 142, December 1977; R. Adams, 'Competing Paradigms in Industrial Relations', *Relations Industrielles* **38**, 3, 1983, 508–31; J. Barbash, *The Elements of Industrial Relations*, Madison, Wisc., University of Wisconsin Press, 1984, 3–33, 130–6; A. Blain, & J. Gennard, 'Industrial Relations Theory: A Critical Review', *British Journal of Industrial Relations* **8**, November 1970, 387–407; A. Craig, *The System of Industrial Relations in Canada*, 3rd edn, Scarborough, Ont., Prentice-Hall, 1990, chap. 1, 1–19; Braham Dabscheck, 'Of Mountains and Routes Over Them: A Survey of Theories of Industrial Relations', *Journal of Industrial Relations* **25**, 4, December 1983, 485–506; S. Dimmock & A. Sethi, 'The Role of Ideology and Power in Systems Theory: Some Fundamental Shortcomings', *Relations Industrielles* **41**, 4, 1986, 738–55; A. Giles & G. Murray. 'The Rise and Fall of the Systems Approach: Implications for an Understanding of Canadian Industrial Relations', *Proceedings of the 24th Annual Meeting of the Canadian Industrial Relations Association*, June 1987, 617–36; J. Goodman, E. Armstrong, A. Wagner, J. Davis & S. Ward, 'Rules in Industrial Relations Theory', *Industrial Relations Journal* **6**, 1, 1975, 14–30; Syed M. A. Hameed, 'A Critique of Industrial Relations Theory', *Relations Industrielles* **37**, 1, 1982, 15–31; T. A. Kochan & H. C. Katz, *Collective Bargaining and Industrial Relations*, 2nd edn, Homewood, Ill., 1988, chapter 1; T. A. Kochan, H. C.

Katz & R. B. McKersie, *The Transformation of American Industrial Relations*, New York, Basic Books, 1986, chapter 4, 81–108; N. M. Meltz, 'The Industrial Relations Systems Model as an Analytical Tool', in Schlomo Maital (ed.), *Applied Behavioural Economics*, Volume II, Brighton, UK, Wheatsheaf, 1988, 613–19; W. K. Roche, 'Systems Analysis and Industrial Relations: Double Paradox in the Development of American and British Industrial Relations Theory', *Economics and Industrial Democracy* **7**, 1986, 3–28; G. Schienstock, 'Towards a Theory of Industrial Relations', *British Journal of Industrial Relations* **191**, July 1981, 170–89; M. Shalev, 'Industrial Relations Theory and the Comparative Study of Industrial Relations and Industrial Conflict', *British Journal of Industrial Relations* **XVIII**, 1, March 1980, 26–41; R. Singh, 'Systems Theory in the Study of Industrial Relations: Time For a Re-appraisal', *Industrial Relations Journal* **7**, Autumn 1976, 59–71; Kenneth Walker, 'Towards Useful Theorising About Industrial Relations', *British Journal of Industrial Relations* **XV**, 3, November 1977, 307–16; and S. Wood, A. Wagner, E. Armstrong, J. Goodman & J. Davis, 'The Industrial Relations System Concept as a Basis for Theory in Industrial Relations', *British Journal of Industrial Relations* **13**, 3, 1975, 291–308.

3   The omitted sections refer to the economic system which Dunlop identifies as requiring the same approach as an industrial relations system.

4   Dunlop usually refers to work place and work community. This double reference is presumably intended to distinguish between the micro work environment and the larger community within which there is a diversity of work places.

5   In a letter to the author, dated 30 October 1989, Dunlop makes the following comments on the author's point that there is a confusing use of the term 'rules' for both the process of resolving disputes and the specific terms of employment:

> I have difficulty in understanding how it is confusing to use rules to refer, as I do, to both substance and process, to rules relating to compensation, movement of workers, discipline, etc. as well as to grievance procedure, renewal of provisions, etc. The railroad example (p. 22) is perfectly clear that the term covers both. Indeed, as you well know, substantive rules and process are deeply intertwined in any relationship, whether one is talking about a sectoral system within the United States or thinking of a comparison of national systems.

6   While Dunlop is often said to have referred to a 'shared ideology', I don't believe he actually uses this expression. He refers to a common ideology on p. 17. On p. 16 in footnote 20, he credits Clark Kerr as suggesting the term 'shared understanding'.

7   There are other criticisms such as this not really being a true systems model. This criticism seems irrelevant in terms of the objective of usefulness set out by Dunlop. The question is whether the model works, not whether or not it is a true systems model.

References

Adams, Roy J. 1988. Desperately seeking industrial relations theory. *International Journal of Comparative Labour, Law and Industrial Relations* 4, 1, Spring, 1–10.

Adams, Roy J. 1989. The Hardest Course: Teaching Comparative Industrial Relations. Prepared for the Study Group on Industrial Relations Theory, IIRA Eighth World Congress, Post Congress Workshop, Brussels, Belgium, 8 September.

Craig, Alton, W. J. 1986. *The System of Industrial Relations in Canada*, 2nd edition, Scarborough, Ont.: Prentice-Hall.

Dunlop, John T. 1958. *Industrial Relations Systems*. New York: Henry Holt.

Kochan, Thomas A., Harry C. Katz, & Robert B. McKersie 1986. *The Transformation of American Industrial Relations*. New York: Basic Books.

Meltz, Noah M. 1989. Why are there few academic industrial relations departments? Prepared for the Study Group on Industrial Relations Theory, IIRA Eighth World Congress, Post Congress Workshop, Brussels, Belgium, 8 September.

3 John R. Commons and the Western industrial relations tradition

JACK BARBASH

This is a chapter on John R. Commons as *a*, if not *the*, founding father of industrial relations in the United States. Industrial relations as used here is the field of study and practice that deals with the resolution of conflict in the employment relationship. Commons is compared with Marx, Mayo, Taylor and the Webbs who are treated as co-founders of Western industrial relations, all reacting to the economists' analysis of labour.

The premiss here is that a field of study needs to have a sense of its origins, fundamental ideas, and values. Commons was the first American to articulate the premisses of industrial relations as the United States was becoming a great industrial power; he then undertook to suit theory to policy, in the meantime training a generation to do likewise.

For all his seminal importance Commons is hardly known outside of the United States and even there he has, with time, become a rather dim figure. I deal with Commons as practitioner–theorist and as the great embodiment of the unity of practice and theory. The effort here is to understand Commons on his own terms not to make a critical analysis. It is enough to note simply that he was controversial in his own time and in posterity's judgement.

Life and times

John R. Commons is best known as a professor at the University of Wisconsin around the first third of the twentieth century. The whole fabric of social and labour legislation in the United States bears his indelible imprint and that of his students and collaborators.

Commons and company have made landmark contributions to apprenticeship, vocational education, workers' compensation, job safety, factory inspection, social security, unemployment compensation, unionism, collective bargaining, civil service, and, not least, to the administration of labour law.

Joseph Dorfman said of Commons that 'more than any other economist he was responsible for the conversion into public policy of reform proposals designed to alleviate defects in the industrial system' (Dorfman 1959: 377). Kenneth Boulding said, 'Commons was the intellectual origin of the New Deal, of labor legislation, of social security, of the whole movement in the country toward a welfare state' (Boulding 1956: 7).

Commons came to maturity in the progressive era of American history:

> that . . . impulse toward criticism and change that was everywhere
> so conspicuous after 1900 when the already forceful stream of
> agrarian discontent was enlarged and redirected by the growing
> enthusiasm of middle class people for social and economic reform.
> (Hofstader 1955: 5)

Progressivism's great monuments were Theodore Roosevelt's Square Deal and Woodrow Wilson's New Freedom. Commons's own base of operations was Wisconsin in the time of a third seminal Progressive, Robert M. La Follette. Commons was 'born again' when he came to the 'thrilling state' of Wisconsin (Commons 1934: 5). La Follette 'opened up . . . a noble idea of patriotism for the State wherein there should be no corruption in politics, no control of governors and legislatures by the lobbyists of corporations, no machine controlling the party conventions. Instead there should be a resurrection of the early American idealism of government by the people themselves' (Commons 1964: 98). The Governor La Follette and the Professor Commons became collaborators in the 'Wisconsin idea': a partnership of the 'State Government . . . [in] instruction, research, extension [and] economics' (Commons 1964: 97).

Wisconsin in this period became a great state laboratory for social innovation.

Commons tells his own life story:

> My first introduction to the problem of the relations of law
> to economics was in the classes of Professor [Richard T.]
> Ely at Johns Hopkins University, 1888. In 1899 I investigated,
> for the United States Industrial Commission, the subject of
> immigration, which took me to the headquarters of practically
> all the national trade unions. This led to a further investigation
> of restrictions of output by capitalistic and labor organizations.
> After 1901 I participated in labor arbitration with the National
> Civic Federation, representing 'labor, employers, and the public,'
> and, in 1906, with the same organization, in an investigation of
> municipal and private operations of public utilities ... In 1905
> I drafted a civil service law and in 1907 a public utility law ...
> In 1906 and 1907, I investigated with others, for the Russell Sage
> Foundation, labor conditions in the steel industry at Pittsburgh.
> During 1910 and 1911, when the Socialists were in control of the
> City of Milwaukee, I organized for them a Bureau of Economy and
> Efficiency. In 1911 I drafted, and then participated for two years
> in the administration of, an Industrial Commission law for the
> State of Wisconsin, with the purpose of ascertaining and enforcing
> reasonable rules and practices in the relations between employers
> and employees. From 1913 to 1915 I was a member of the Industrial
> Relations Commission appointed by President Wilson. In 1923 I
> represented [with others] four western states before the Federal
> Trade Commission on the Pittsburgh Plus case of discrimination
> practices by the United States Steel Corporation ... Between 1924
> and 1926, I administered for two years, as chairman, a voluntary
> plan of unemployment insurance in the clothing industry of
> Chicago. This plan was similar to that which I had previously
> devised in 1923, for legislation. The plan with improvements, was
> finally enacted in Wisconsin in 1932. (Commons 1934: 2–3)

Add Commons's active role in the American Association for Labor
Legislation, the most significant lobbying organization for labour
legislation of its time.

Commons's works

Commons employed conservative means to achieve radical aims.
His conservatism sprang from an assessment of American society
as essentially conservative, and likely from his own temperament as

well. His radical aim was the creative use of government to alleviate injustice in the employment relationship, an end which, it was clear to him, the market alone could not accomplish. Neither could it be safely left to the conventional radicals.

Commons's conservatism of means sought to make state intervention compatible with American individualism by (a) working within capitalism; (b) professionalizing the administration of the labour law to insulate it against politics as usual; (c) applying a rule of reasonableness to enforcement; (d) relying on state rather than federal power; (e) encouraging voluntarism to alleviate social injustice; (f) involving the parties at interest in the legislative and administrative process; and (g) introducing change gradually.

Commons wanted 'to save capitalism by making it good' (Commons [1924] 1959: 143). The profit motive could be used 'to promote the welfare of the whole community by giving employers incentives to comply with the labor legislation' (Commons 1934: 60). Commons designed unemployment compensation 'to induce the employer to *prevent* unemployment instead of only a *relief* measure' (Commons 1934: 842; italics in original).

Commons followed the same principle in labour relations: he worked with moderate employers to bring other employers around as he did in his mediation work with the National Civil Federation (Harter 1962: 167).

Commons's idea of professionalism was attuned to the progressive spirit of reform: 'not that good and evil did not exist, rather that to diminish evil some sort of "method of intelligence" must be used' (Haber 1964: 54–5).

Bill-drafting demonstrated Commons's method of intelligence in action. Wisconsin was the first state to establish a Legislative Reference Service. 'Before, legislators could look only to lobbyist lawyers to draft bills. Now they could turn to investigators and lawyers paid by the State.' Charles McCarthy, the service's founder, 'had or would get immediately almost everything one might need on all sides . . . This stubborn criticism of every detail forced [Commons] to the most careful self-criticism that I had ever known' (Commons 1964: 109–10). Due process, for Commons, required investigation of 'all the facts in the case . . . before decision is made . . . [and] a hearing in order that all facts be known' (Commons 1919: 16).

But Commons was much more than an early technocrat. The economist's place was that of adviser to the leaders because it is they who have to bear the costs (Commons 1964: 88).

Rather than 'a mere statute administered by a bureaucratic commission', Commons brought the parties at interest into the administrative process through species of tripartism or social contract. 'It is as nearly a voluntary system of collective bargaining as the nature of our constitutional government will permit', he said, describing the Wisconsin Industrial Commission (Commons 1934: 852). Commons sought 'willing obedience by employers' instead of 'resentful antagonism' and a change in attitude by the state 'from prosecution for crime to collaboration in working out, along with representatives of labor, improvements in labor conditions' (Commons 1934: xxviii).

Commons was an incrementalist. 'Too much progressivism and radicalism at a single dose' brings political reaction (Commons in Dorfman 1959: 379). He was an opportunist, he said, 'pushed into danger by experimentation. If physical scientists risk their lives in experiments why should not an economic scientist risk his job' (Commons 1964: 48).

Commons's voluntarism worked on the principle that government, even though essential, was only one of several institutions that had to be enlisted in the cause of equity for working people. Private institutions like trade unions, collective bargaining or 'industrial government' as he called it, and employer personnel administration must also serve.

Reasonableness is a recurring word in Commons's vocabulary. Utopias sound good but are unenforceable. 'Reasonableness', Commons said, is 'idealism enforced by practicality' which could be 'investigated and ascertained as actually in operation' (Commons 1964: 156).

Commons's preference for a state labour policy stemmed less from any strong conviction about states' rights than from his own successful experience with the Wisconsin idea, symbolizing thus Louis D. Brandeis's notion of the states as 'laboratories of democracy'. Nor was there, in any event, a body of federal experience with social and labour policy which Commons could have turned to for most of his career.

Commons's conservatism in pursuit of a radical end was, in my view, a strategy to Americanize – so to speak – the labour problem away from its negative European contexts for most Americans, of socialism, class war, Marxism, and revolution, and from what we think of today as a welfare state (Barbash 1967). Commons's incrementalism, professionalism, bargaining, 'class collaboration', pro-capitalism, and power dispersion were aimed at gaining consent of the chief actors and thereby defusing the likely explosive reactions to his social justice–equity goals. Commons's 'American exceptionalism' (not his term, by the way) argued that American labour movements have risen from native soil qualitatively different from the European experience (Commons & Andrews [1916] 1936: 3).

Commons's theory

'No antagonism between theory and practice' existed for Commons. 'A theory is only a tool for investigating practice, like a spade for digging up facts and converting them into an understandable system' (Commons 1934: 722). Commons's theory came from 'participation in collective activities' (Commons 1934: 1) as printer, trade unionist, mediator, administrator, bill drafter, investigator, professor, and teacher. His theory was fundamentally rooted in a religious upbringing which led him very early to speak out against injustice.

Commons was not at his best as a rigorous theorist. But it is none the less possible to distil a structure of his ideas from his voluminous writings without doing violence to the animating spirit.

The labour problem begins for Commons with 'the peculiar nature of labor as a commodity' (Commons & Andrews [1916] 1936: 1). Unlike other commodities, labour has a 'soul' (Commons 1919: 20). The human mind was not 'a passive receptacle of ideas; it was capable of making choices . . . manipulating the external world' rather than being manipulated by it (Commons 1934: 16–17).

For employers labour is primarily a cost and therefore, like any other commodity, its use must be governed by supply and demand in the labour market. The engineer sees labour as a piece of machinery subject to the laws of efficiency (Commons 1919: 14). These approaches are valid in their contexts but incomplete. They fail to take into account what Commons called the worker's goodwill; what others would later call morale and job satisfaction.

The worker's goodwill 'enlists the whole soul and all [the worker's] energies in the things he is doing. It . . . cannot be broken up and measured off in motions and parts of motions for it is not science but personality. It is the unity of a living being.' Labour's goodwill is not only individual 'self-interest'. It is also 'labor's solidarity of interest' or what the French call 'l'esprit de corps' (Commons 1919: 19–20).

The relationship between the 'propertyless seller of himself on the one hand and a propertied buyer on the other' creates an inequality of bargaining power because the worker is under the 'imperious necessity of immediately agreeing with the employer'. The courts and the economists misperceived the individual worker and his employer as equal when, in reality, they are basically unequal (Commons & Andrews [1916] 1936: 1). It was the narrowing of this inequality which engaged Commons's entire career.

Commons looked to the resolution of inequality by the state, by employees on their own and in their unions, and by the employer. State legislation under democracy and equal suffrage had to be the primaryy source (Commons & Andrews [1916] 1936: 1). 'Legislation goes beyond the legal face of things and looks' at the real bargaining relationship The elected legislators are able to recognize that the labour bargain is not only about wages: in a very real sense wages are 'about life itself'. Corrective legislation like health and safety, minimum wages, unions and collective bargaining to protect life needs to be enacted. Commons called for 'a new equity' – an equity that will 'protect the job as the older equity protected the business' (Commons [1924] 1959: 307), meaning standards and procedures to protect the workers' human condition.

The workers themselves are not altogether powerless to resist the weakening of their human condition. There is, to begin with, the 'basic solidarity of interest' which brings workers to socialize their resistance to efficiency measures. Workers resist engineering efficiency by restriction of output. Even without a union 'the labourer is bargaining while he is at work and his tacit offer to the employers is the amount of work he is turning out' (Commons 1919: 15–23 passim).

Beyond restriction of output modern industry creates conditions which institutionalize employee defences in the form of unions. Unions engage in collective bargaining to establish rules of equity in the work place. Commons remembered how 'in the non–union [printing] office the foreman was a dictator. He had his "pets" to whom he gave his steady work; and he gave them the "fat", meaning the kind of work that paid better wages than other kinds of work . . . But in the union office the foreman was restrained in these matters by rules agreed on by the labor union and the owners of the newspaper' (Commons 1950: ch. 1).

The union is basically a protective institution which necessarily restricts employer freedom. If it 'direct[ed] its energies to the

production of wealth ... it would insofar cease to be a trade
union and would become either a society for technical education
or an association for sharing profits, or a co-operative association'
(Commons 1923: 122). All of which unions had experimented with
but eventually abandoned.

The evolution of union governmental forms from the shop all the
way to the national and international union has been shaped by
the expansion of markets for the goods produced by its members.
National unions spring from national markets. In its highest form
collective bargaining was 'industrial government with its legislative,
executive and judicial branches, its common law and statute law, its
penalties and sanctions' (Commons 1921: vii), as Commons's historic
research revealed.

Scarcity necessarily generated useful conflicts of interest over
relative shares but these conflicts can be resolved through bargaining.
Bargaining begins with conflict but it is 'mutual dependence' which
brings the parties to bargain and create order out of conflict and
'harmony of interests'.

Harmony is not foreordained. It arises out of a bargaining
transaction with each party free to withhold what the other side
wants. Withholding makes it a relationship between equals which
contrasts with managerial and rationing transactions which are
necessarily relationships among unequals (Commons 1934: 55, 93).
Collective bargaining not only applies to the terms of employment and
rules in the work place but extends as well to public policy. Given the
complexity imposed by the human essence of labour, the collective
agreement becomes more than a spot transaction; it is a 'constitution
for industrial government' (Common [1924] 1959: 312).

'Wage-conscious' rather than 'class-conscious' unionism was better adapted to the American environment (Commons & Associates
1918: Vol. 1, 15). Socialism is fundamentally alien to the worker's
own psychology which focuses on job rights, 'shorter hours of
labor, freedom to escape from economic oppression', rather than
socialism's 'higher idealism' of owning the means of production
(Commons 1923: 49–50). The union already has enough to do
to survive in a hostile society. Taking on socialism adds an extra
jeopardy.

It is in the employer's own interest to recognize the importance
of employee goodwill in promoting efficiency 'because it brings
larger profits and lifts the employer somewhat above the level of
competing employers by giving him a more productive labor force'

(Commons 1919: 26). Later this approach came to be known as human relations. The emerging personnel departments 'deal with every human relation within and without the establishment. It is the department of justice as well as the department of health and efficiency' (Commons 1919: 105).

Commons's method

Commons carried on much of his research as researcher-investigator and 'participant-observer'. The investigator not only observes but participates too in order to get inside of the situation he is investigating (Wilber 1978: 372).

Commons was trained as an economist. But he found that the state–of–the–art in economics was too confining and too abstract to explain economic behaviour and to serve as the theory of economics in action.

Commons was 'multi–disciplinary' – we would say today – employing history, sociology, social psychology, and particularly law for the fuller illumination of economic behaviour. His greatest works were in the fields of history ('American Shoemakers, 1648–1895', *Documentary History of American Industrial Society* and *The History of Labor in the United States*) and law (*Legal Foundations of Capitalism*).

Commons transcended a dull speaking style to become a great teacher. Edwin E. Witte, who became the 'father' of American social security, remembered how Commons's students came to his classes as rebels; they came away wanting 'to improve what ... was wrong but without destroying our political, economic and social structure', to 'know the facts ...' to think in terms of remedies rather than criticisms and to learn from the people directly interested'. Commons taught 'by example' rather than by 'preaching' (Witte in Harter 1962: 77–8).

David J. Saposs, a co–author of the monumental *History*, recalled years later how Commons 'aroused our curiosity and broadened our horizons through his analytical mind and provocative ideas' (Saposs 1960: 10–11). Selig Perlman saw Commons as an 'intellectual democrat'. He asked 'genuine groping questions without any definite goal – a mere stabbing in this direction and in that ... and then ... a question or a series of questions would come forth which ... touched the nerve of the situation' (Perlman 1950: 5). Frank P.

Walsh, the chairman of the US Commission on Industrial Relations, who otherwise sharply disagreed with Commons, described him as a 'pygmy physically but a giant when it comes to intellect' and 'the most accomplished political economist of his time' (Walsh 1966: 69).

Commons in context

Commons's key concepts are equity, bargaining, reasonableness, pragmatism, and institutionalism. By equity Commons meant fairness for employees. Bargaining best achieves equity in the work place because the parties deal with each other from a position of equality rather than from command and obedience (Commons 1934: 52 ff).

Reasonableness tempers bargaining power with intelligence, reason, and common sense. Commons favoured pragmatism or experience over utopianism in formulating policy. 'Let us investigate and [then] come to an understanding as to what should and can be done' (Commons 1934: 117).

Commons was an institutional economist. Individuals functioned economically mainly through unions, corporations, law, etc. Mainline economics, on the other hand, 'in imitation of the physical sciences treated the individual like atoms, molecules' (Commons 1950: 15). It was not that Commons was anti-market – he was not – it was that as an institutionalist he 'assigned a major role in the allocation and pricing of labor to non-market forces' (Segal 1986: 389).

Commons was a product of his times in several senses. He was an American – 'a son of the middle border' (Chamberlain. 1964). His time was the era of craft union islands and open shops in a stormy sea of employer repression and labour injunctions. The progressive era stirred hopes of change for Commons and many others.

Much of Commons's work is a running commentary on the prevailing theories and doctrines. His institutional economics – 'collective action in control, liberation and expansion of individual action' (Commons 1950: 1) – challenged the individualistic assumptions of mainline economics and their anti-social effects.

Co-founders

The work of Commons, Marx, Mayo, Taylor and the Webbs, as it intersects with economics, stands for me as the foundation of

Western industrial relations. Like Commons, the other founders combined the scientific quest for an intellectual system with a reformer's zeal in bringing it to life.

Marx and Mayo, like Commons, start with the premiss that the labour problem begins with labour's human essence. Classical economics understood this too, but treated labour as a deviant case. Each, in his own fashion – Commons, Marx, Taylor, and Mayo – treats labour as his general case and builds on it.

The foundation of Marx's system is the theory of surplus value: human labour is unique among the factors of production in being able to produce more than it costs. The worker 'is more than a mere item in the cost of production', Mayo said (Mayo [1919] 1970: 131). He is a 'citizen fulfilling a social function' (Mayo 1945: 50). Mayo rejects the hyper-rationality, economism and individualism central to economics and denounces the 'anomie' inflicted by modern industrial organization.

Taylor set forth a 'machinery' theory of labour, as Commons said (Commons 1919: 7–17). Taylor's work established the efficient utilization of labour as a central function of Western capitalist industrialism and eventually, as it turned out, of socialist industrialism as well. Taylor's 'machinery' theory provides grist for Mayo's anomie indictment and Commons's criticism of its impersonality.

Commons, Marx and Mayo deal with what Marxists call the social relations of production going beyond economics' treatment of labour as a factor of production, albeit the human factor (McNulty 1980: 107 ff). But their diverse analyses of social relations lead them to diverse roads to equity. Commons's equity is served by bargaining if the parties stand in a proximate relationship of equality. Mayo seems to rely on management's enlightened self-interest reacting to employee restriction of output.

Unions' collective bargaining and conflict are not as legitimate for Mayo and Taylor as they are for Commons and Marx. Mayo stressed collaboration; conflict is a 'social disease' (Mayo [in Bendix & Fisher] 1949: 314). Taylor's science could not tolerate collective negotiations and, indeed, his *Scientific Management* is an anti-union tract. Unions are important to Marx but mainly as waystations to socialism. For Commons unions are worthy and useful ends in their own right and conflict in industrial relations is normal not pathological.

Adversarialism is central to Commons and Marx. But Marx's unremitting class struggle under capitalism runs counter to Commons's mediation of class conflict through equity. Class has its uses as an analytical tool for Commons but its thrust is blunted for him by divisiveness *within* the classes. Commons identifies an essential common ground between management and employees which Marx rejects. Commons rejects socialism outright as an equity option. In particular: the dictatorship exercised by state or party is at odds with Commons's diffusion of power.

Taylor's scientific management is 'fair' because 'under scientific management arbitrary power, arbitrary dictatorship ceases; and ... every single subject, large and small, becomes the question for scientific investigation, for reduction to law' (Taylor [1911] 1947: 212). This view was applauded by many progressives of the time who took Taylor at his word that he was, in fact, bringing science to management. But Taylor's brand of elite technocracy runs against Commons's negotiation – which Taylor's disciples later come around to. Mayo's human relations derived its *raison d'être* as a protest against Taylorism's brand of science, although neo-human relations is frequently presented as 'behavioral science'.

Commons and the Webbs

The Webbs are reserved for special handling here because they occupy a large common ground with Commons in the treatment of unions and collective bargaining. To begin with, the Webbs provided Commons with a model of academic scholarship in treating the labour problem (Commons 1964: 71).

'The Webbs', Leonard Woolf observed, ' ... did not merely analyse and dissect ... the trade unions .. in *The History of Trade Unionism* and *Industrial Democracy*. It is almost true that they not only discovered but invented them.' Before the Webbs 'neither governments, nor civil servants, nor politicians, nor trade unionists themselves understood ... what the form of the trade union movement was, what it had achieved and what its functions had been and might be' (Woolf 1949: 254).

In the same sense Commons also 'discovered' trade unionism and tried to understand it on its own terms. Commons and the Webbs shared, too, the aversion to the abstractions of economics and Marxism in dealing with unions and labour.

Commons and the Webbs were doers. 'Sidney Webb's first thought in dealing with any question that he took up was to find an administratively workable solution' (Cole 1956: 210). Commons,

I have been saying, represented the unity of theory and practice. The Webbs never returned to industrial relations after *Industrial Democracy*. Commons never left industrial relations and trained and educated a legion of disciples to continue on where he had left off – which they did.

With all of Commons's difficulties with theory his work is, none the less, informed by a basic theory and philosophy. Sidney Webb had 'no underlying philosophy"; Beatrice was probably 'much more of a philosopher' (Cole 1956: 210).

But the Webbs did schematize trade unions and collective bargaining into enduring categories: the methods of mutual insurance, legal enactment and arbitration (Webb & Webb [1897] 1914: 703–807); the trade union 'expedients' of the 'common rule – the restriction of numbers' and the 'standard rate' (Webb & Webb [1894] 1920: 1); and defined the union in classic terms as a 'continuous association of wage earners for the purpose of monitoring or improving the conditions of their working lives' (Webb & Webb [1894] 1920: 1).

Commons and the Webbs differed in role conception. Commons brought an American populist outlook to social policy. The technician played only a supporting part to the politician, trade unionist and businessman who had to make the final decisions (Commons 1964: 86). For the Webbs, their research provided them 'with the material for permeating and persuading practical men to do what the Webbs thought ought to be done or for blowing them up [hyperbole of course] if they refused to be permeated or persuaded' (Woolf 1949: 259).

A synthesis?

Despite differences, the founders have established a coherent intellectual tradition for Western industrial relations with a central purpose – the enforcement of fairness or equity in the employment relationship (Barbash 1988). Equity is deemed labour's due, labour being seen as the human element in production, as the weaker party, and, most recently, as a necessary condition of management efficiency.

The distinguishing feature of Western industrial relations is the ability of unions and management to negotiate their terms of employment with a large measure of freedom from the state compared to the state's dominant position in the socialist and newly industrialized systems. Economists have pretty much made their case that a market system is necessary to keep industrial relations' equity outcomes within the bounds of competitiveness. Economics has also made its case that a strong market system is probably indispensable to an industrial democracy.

The history of industrial relations as a field begins with Marx because he was the first to comprehend capitalism and its labour process as a system and to raise fundamental questions about its equity. For contemporary industrial relations mainline economics, despite shortcomings in detail, has defined the overarching constraints which keep industrial relations within the bounds of competitiveness. Economics seems also to have established as given that an advanced capitalist market system represents the most favourable habitat for equity in the employment relationship.

Max Weber's rationality (which we have not discussed here), Taylor's application of the rationality principle through scientific management, and Mayo's human relations have established the major points of reference for management's administration of the labour process. But rationality and scientific management in the employment relationship, if unregulated, lead to Marx's exploitation and alienation, and by another route to Mayo's (and Durkheim's) anomie, unless arrested by Mayo's human relations and by the unions, collective bargaining and legal enactments of Commons and the Webbs. Commons and the Webbs also make the point that it isn't only the employer who confronts employees; divisions within the working class and the union may position groups of employees to confront one another.

The intellectual tradition allows room for variation within Western industrial relations: the limited state intervention and non–socialist unionism of Commons, the social democracy of the Webbs, and, finally, the non- or anti–union human relations of Mayo – the last reinforced by mainline economics' view of unions and collective bargaining – as either irrelevant or dysfunctional.

References

Barbash, Jack 1967. John R. Commons and the Americanization of the labor problem. *Journal of Economic Issues* **I**, 3, September, 161–7.
Barbash, Jack 1988. Industrial relations and the idea of equity. Paper to the International Industrial Relations Association, Congress of the Americas, Quebec.

Boulding, Kenneth 1956. 'A new look at institutionalism. *American Economic Review: Papers and Proceedings*. Menash, Wisc.
Chamberlain, Neil W. 1965. The institutional economics of John R. Commons. In *Institutional Economics*, C. E. Ayres, *et al.* (eds). Berkeley & Los Angeles, Calif.: University of California.
Cole, G. D. H. *The Second International*. Vol. III: *A History of Socialist Thought*. London: Macmillan.
Commons, John R. 1919. *Industrial Goodwill*. New York: McGraw–Hill.
Commons, John R. 1921. *Trade Unionism and Labor Problems*. Boston, Mass.: Ginn.
Commons, John R. 1923. *Labor and Administration*. New York: Macmillan.
Commons, John R. [1924] 1959. *Legal Foundations of Capitalism*. Madison, Wisc.: University of Wisconsin.
Commons, John R. 1934. *Institutional Economics*. New York: Macmillan.
Commons, John R. 1950. *The Economics of Collective Action*. New York: Macmillan.
Commons, John R. 1964. *Myself*. Madison, Wisc.: University of Wisconsin Press.
Commons, John R. & John B. Andrews [1916] 1936. *Principles of Labor Legislation*, 4th edn. New York: Harper.
Commons, John R. & associates 1918. *History of Labor in the United States*. Vol. 1. New York: Macmillan.
Dorfman, Joseph 1959. *The Economic Mind in America 1918–1933*. New York: Viking.
Haber, Samuel 1964. *Efficiency and Uplift*. Chicago: University of Chicago Press.
Harter, L. B. 1962. *John R. Commons*. Corvallis, Oreg.: Oregon University Press.
Hofstader, Richard 1955. *The Age of Reform*. New York: Knopf.
McNulty, Paul J. 1980. *The Origins and Development of Labor Economics*. Cambridge, Mass.: MIT Press.
Mayo, Elton [1919] 1970. Social growth and social disintegration. In *Readings in Management*, Ernest Dale (ed.), p. 131. New York: McGraw-Hill.
Mayo, Elton 1945. *The Social Problems of an Industrial Civilization*. Boston, Mass.: Harvard University Press.
Mayo, Elton 1949. Quoted in Reinhard Bendix & Lloyd Fisher. The perspectives of Elton Mayo. *Review of Economics and Statistics* **31**, 4, November, 314.
Perlman, Selig 1950. John Rogers Commons, 1862–1945. In *Economics of Collective Action*, John R. Commons (ed.), p. 5. New York: Macmillan.
Saposs, David J. 1960. The Wisconsin heritage and the study of labor – words and deeds of John R. Commons. In *University of Wisconsin School for Workers: 35th Anniversary Papers*, 10–11. Madison, Wisc.: University of Wisconsin Press, July.
Segal, Martin 1986. Post-institutionalism in labor economics – the forties and fifties revisited. *Industrial and Labor Relations Review* **39**, 3, April, 389.
Taylor, Frederick W. [1911] 1947. *Scientific Management*. New York: Harper.
Walsh, Frank P. 1966. Quoted in *Age of Industrial Violence, 1910–1915*,

Graham Adams Jr (ed.). New York: Columbia University Press.
Webb, Beatrice & Sidney Webb [1894] 1920. *The History of Trade Unionism*. London: Longmans Green.
Webb, Beatrice & Sidney Webb [1897] 1914. *Industrial Democracy*. London: Longmans Green.
Wilber, Charles K. & Robert S. Harrison 1978. The methodological basis of institutional economics. *Journal of Economic Issues* **XII**, 1, March, 75.
Witte, Edwin E. 1962. Remarks at John R. Commons' birthday dinner, October 10, 1950. In *John R. Commons*, L. B. Harter (ed.), 77–8. Corvallis, Oreg.: Oregon State University Press.
Woolf, Leonard 1949. Political thought and the Webbs. In *The Webbs and Their Work* Margaret Cole (ed.), 254–9. London: Frederick Muller.

Additional references

Barbash, Jack 1976. The legal foundations of capitalism and the labor problem. *Journal of Economic Issues* **X**, 4, December, 799–810.
Barbash, Jack 1981. Theories of the labor movement in their institutional setting. *Journal of Economic Issues* **XV**, 2, June, 299–309.
A bibliography of the writings of John R. Commons, 1950. In *Economics of Collective Action*, John R. Commons (ed.), 377–408. New York: Macmillan.
Dorfman, Joseph *et al.* 1964. *Institutional Economics*. Berkeley, Calif.: University of California Press.
Miller, Harold L. 1986. *The John R. Commons Papers*. Madison, Wisc.: State Historical Society of Wisconsin.
Parsons, Kenneth 1942. John R. Commons' point of view. *Journal of Land and Public Utility Economics* **XVIII**, 3, August, 245–66.
Perlman, Mark 1958. *Labor Union Theories in America*. Evanston, Ill.: Row, Peterson.
Selekman, Benjamin M. 1959. An economics for administrators. In *A Moral Philosophy for Management*, Benjamin M. Selekman (ed.), 121–33. New York: McGraw-Hill.
Taft, Philip 1952. Theories of the labor movement. In *Interpreting the Labor Movement*, G. W. Brooks *et al.* (eds). Madison, Wisc.: Industrial Relations Research Association.·

4 *The comparative analysis of union growth*

ROBERT PRICE

Since the earliest days of trade unions there has been a continuing interest by commentators in the course of union membership growth and decline. By far the most popular approach has been to link the trajectory of union organization to economic factors. Commons's analysis of American union membership trends in the nineteenth century probably represents the earliest extended presentation of the argument that union growth and activity are closely linked to economic performance (Commons & Associates 1918). The Wisconsin team advanced the view that union membership would grow in the upswing of the 'business cycle', due to the combined effects of greater employer ability to make concessions to organized labour, and greater worker pressure for concessions. In the downswing, the Wisconsin view was that union membership was likely to decline for precisely the opposite reasons; employers would enjoy less room for manoeuvre, and workers would be less inclined to press for increases. In some cases, the downswing would also lead to an upsurge in political agitation, as unfulfilled economic demands were pursued through political activity.

The imprecision of the argument is self-evident. How quickly does union membership respond to the fluctuations of the economy? Does a given value of economic change always produce a similar value for membership change? If not, what other factors account for the variations in response? What explains the resort to political agitation at some economic conjunctures, but not at others? The rudimentary tools of analysis available to these early scholars make such imprecision inevitable and understandable. But as a general proposition, the link between union recruiting success and economic prosperity in the United States up to the end of the second decade of the century was widely accepted (Bain & Elsheikh 1976).

A very similar stance was adopted by the main British writers on trade unions in the late nineteenth and early twentieth centuries, Sidney and Beatrice Webb (Webb & Webb 1894).

Comparative analysis of the course of union membership in the four main Western economies up to the mid-1930s by Davis pointed to a closer association between rising prices and union growth, than between 'prosperity' and growth. Davis, however, went on to argue that both the prosperity and price theories of union growth were too simple. His central conclusion was that the most favourable periods for union membership growth were those 'when labor has major new grievances and an improving position in the labor market' (Davis 1941: 615). This proposition reflected the dominant economistic and defensive conception of union objectives that characterized early Anglo-American analysis. This qualified version of the 'business cycle' theory marks an important step in the evolution of union growth theory, but its imprecision is equally evident. Davis himself entered a number of significant additional qualifications that blurred the apparent clarity of his basic theoretical proposition. He made much of the need for union leaders to respond effectively to favourable recruitment conditions; he argued that government support could make a significant difference to the size of any upsurge in union membership; and he pointed to the impact of employer intimidation and 'welfare' policies in reducing unions' capacity to recruit. Indeed, the final sentence of his 1941 article suggests that these latter factors would become more significant in determining the trend of union growth than the essentially economic conditions that had been important for growth in the past. 'Today, not only the growth but even the existence of the unions has become in large measure a political problem (1941: 633).

This shift of emphasis was mirrored in the key theoretical analyses of the early postwar decades. While economic factors were accepted as important influences on short-term fluctuations in membership, the dominant factors in determining long-term trends were identified by a number of writers as essentially sociopolitical. Dunlop's work on industrial relations systems stressed the key role of 'the system of law and the ethos and beliefs of the community' in the long-term evolution of the unions (Dunlop 1948). Bernstein, in similar vein, argued the importance of 'social acceptability' of unionism, and the role of union security agreements in stabilizing membership (Bernstein 1954). In Britain, Flanders took a similar line with his analytical distinction between periods of 'movement' and of 'organization' in the growth of membership. While economic factors might encourage workers to join unions, it was the underpinning of that growth by employer recognition, union security, and government support for collective bargaining which would determine the course of union membership over the long term (Flanders 1970). While these arguments were clearly capable of generating testable propositions for cross-country comparisons, comparative analyses were rare and lacking in rigour, largely, one suspects, because of the difficulty involved in bringing together large amounts of qualitative and subjective data from under-researched areas of social history.

The advent of computer-based regression analysis regenerated the earlier 'economic' explanations of union growth. Econometric analyses for individual countries (for example, Hines 1964, Ashenfelter & Pencavel 1969), and the four-country comparative analysis of Bain & Elsheikh (1976) all produced correlations accounting for a high proportion of the year-on-year fluctuations in union membership. The economic variables used to explain patterns of growth are inevitably predetermined by the available statistical series; thus, regular appearances are made among the independent variables by prices, wages, unemployment, profits and, of course, union membership itself – all of which are collected as a matter of course by most national statistical bureaux. Nevertheless, the close correspondence between the available series and the factors proposed by the early 'business cycle' and 'price movements' theorists, has meant that modern analysis has been able to build upon and elaborate the deductive reasoning which characterized those early explanations of union membership growth.

In the comparative analysis undertaken by Bain and Elsheikh for Australia, Sweden, Britain and the United States from 1893 to 1970, between 68 and 80 per cent of the annual variation in membership levels is accounted for by the rate of change of prices, the rate of change of money wages, the level and rate of change of unemployment, and the level of union density (1976: 107). The authors explore the underlying patterns of causation in a way that is reminiscent of the work of Commons and Davis. Prices are argued to affect both the propensity to unionize through the threat to workers' real incomes, and the opportunity to unionize through the greater readiness of employers to concede wage rises in a period of rising product prices. Wages are argued to have a positive effect on growth via the credit which unions gain from achieving wage increases, and a negative effect through the dissuasion exercised by increasing real wages.

Table 4.1   Union density rates in OECD countries 1970 and 1985.

	1970	1985
Australia	50.5	51.2
Austria	62.1	58.2
Belgium	67.1	75.8
Denmark	64.3	78.2
France	23.1	18.2*
Germany, West	37.0	36.7
Greece	–	35.5*
Ireland	52.4	46.2
Italy	33.1	40.0*
Japan	35.4	28.9
Netherlands	37.5	29.1
New Zealand	52.7	56.0
Norway	61.8	65.1
Spain	–	21.0
Sweden	80.4	96.3
Switzerland	29.2	32.5
United Kingdom	48.5	43.3
United States	27.2	15.7

* Estimates

Source: R. Price, 'Trade union membership', in *Comparative labour statistics*, R. Bean (ed.), London: Croom Helm, 1989; as with all union membership data, these figures, and those in Table 4.2, have to be heavily qualified as regards accuracy. The main problems of compilation and interpretation are discussed in the chapter from which they are drawn, but for the purposes of this paper, they should be regarded as simply indicative of broad orders of magnitude, and the very wide range of density levels to be found across the OECD countries.

Unemployment will reduce bargaining power and the propensity to unionize if it is high and rising; it will increase union power and unionization rates if it is low or falling. Existing union density levels can either dampen future growth potential via the saturation of the 'market' for union membership, or they can stimulate further growth by the institutionalization of collective bargaining throughout successive sectors of the economy. Bain & Elsheikh argue that, with the exception of the United States between 1937 and 1947 and Australia between 1907 and 1913, the impact of such factors as the law and government action had 'not been sufficiently general or pervasive to be reflected in union growth at the aggregate level' (1976: 86).

This proposition stands in apparent contradiction to the non-quantitatively based theories of the postwar period, which, albeit on the basis of single-country studies, assigned great importance to sociopolitical factors in determining the course of union membership. It also sits uneasily alongside the figures in Table 4.1 which show the massive variation in aggregate union density trends among OECD countries in the mid-1980s.

If economic factors are as powerful an influence on growth as is proposed, would we not expect to find a more homogeneous set of data in countries experiencing similar economic fortunes? Looked at from the reverse perspective, if the business cycle is indeed the key to explaining union growth, what can be said about these countries' experience of economic development that would account for these long-term inter-country differences in density?

I am in the happy position of having been closely associated over the past two decades with research at the University of Warwick that has explored both the economic and the institutional and political factors influencing union growth. Bain's detailed analysis of white-collar union growth in the United Kingdom up to 1964 concluded that

> no significant relationship was found between the growth of aggregate white-collar unionism and such aspects of their economic position as earnings, terms and conditions of employment, employment security. (1970: 183)

The cross-sectional variations in density between industrial sectors in 1964 could be satisfactorily explained by three factors: employment concentration, union recognition, and government action to support collective bargaining at some point in the past. The chapter contributed jointly by Bain and myself to the *Industrial Relations in Britain* textbook (Bain 1983: 3–33) argues for a theory of growth based upon a complex interrelationship between economic forces, employer policies, government action, and personal and job-related characteristics, with the precise contribution of each factor likely to vary widely in different periods (Bain & Price 1983: 33). Neither of these analyses had an international comparative focus, but deploying similar arguments another Warwick scholar, Hugh Clegg, proposed a strong theory to explain the degree of variation in comparative union density levels. In his view, inter-country differences in aggregate density could be explained by the variations between countries in the extent and depth of collective bargaining, the degree of support from employers, and the system for union security (Clegg 1976: 118–19).

The state of the analytical debate is clearly unsatisfactory in a number of important respects. Time-series analysis seems to demonstrate that economic variables have a dominant impact on the rate of change of union membership in some major countries. On the other hand, these economic factors seem to have much less explanatory power in other societies – France and the Netherlands, for example (Visser 1987). But even in those countries where economic factors appear from econometric analysis to have been important, such as Britain, the United States and Sweden, cross-sectional analyses appear to demonstrate that high and low levels of membership and density are associated with a number of key institutional or socio-political factors, not specific economic developments. The issues can be most clearly posed in the form of questions: if the rates of change of prices and unemployment are such powerful influences, why do they affect the private and public service sectors so differently in the United Kingdom? Why should they have affected the public service sector in the United States so differently after 1960 compared with the period before that date? Is it possible to reconcile the contradictory implications of the cross-sectional and time-series approaches?

As far as the cross-sectional approach is concerned, the association of high and low levels of membership with specific institutional features is, in any case, very unsatisfactory as a theoretical statement, since it fails to explain the fundamental question of why state and employer policies should have been so different between countries, or between sectors and industries. Why should the state in the United Kingdom and Sweden have been generally positive towards the development of collective bargaining in the post-war period, while the state in France and Italy was generally lukewarm in its encouragement? Why should employers in Britain have taken a relatively favourable view of white-collar collective bargaining in the 1970s, but an openly hostile view in the 1960s and the 1980s? The variations on this theme are endless, and underline decisively the importance of seeking explanation not simply in association, but in the underlying social and political developments in any country that is being studied.

This discussion has so far failed to take into account two elements that have been particularly prominent in the discussion of union growth and decline in the 1980s. First, much has been made of the changes in the industrial and occupational structures of the industrialized, market economy countries under the impact of technological change and intensified world competition. The shift out of manufacturing into the services sector, increases in unemployment, increased volumes of part-time and temporary work, greater female participation in the labour force have been important features affecting all advanced economies. These elements may obviously influence

year-on-year changes in membership levels within individual countries, and may over time come to account for a significant part
of the variation in unionization between countries. Secondly, the
geographical distribution of employment has been argued to have
an impact both on inter-country differences and on changes over time.
The extent to which employment is concentrated regionally in a few
centres as distinct from being dispersed over large land masses can
affect both worker collective consciousness and union organizational
effectiveness – the United States at one extreme, and Sweden and
Australia at the other, illustrate this point. But the recent period of
technological change has increased the tendency for industrial dispersion in countries like the United Kingdom and the United States,
and may thus have affected the trend rate of growth over time.

Moving forward

The task now confronting analysts of union growth is a daunting one.
We have a healthy stock of studies which clean up the available data for
us; we have any number of econometrically based studies; qualitative
studies of union development over the nearly 50-year period since
the last world war teem with references to growth patterns. How
can we start to integrate the various insights from the theoretical
approaches discussed above with the mass of detailed observations
available in the literature? Can a convincing general and comparative
theoretical approach be developed? A possible analytical framework
is outlined in this section, and in the final section its application to
the growth experiences of the past two decades is discussed.

An important starting-point is to recognize the distinction between
periods of institutional development and periods of institutional
consolidation. Over the long period since the emergence of union
organization in the middle of the nineteenth century, it is evident
that in every country there have been key turning-points that have
radically altered the pattern of institutional arrangements surrounding the employment relationship. The most striking have been those
arising from the social and economic dislocations consequent on the
two world wars; in 1918–20, for example, the Whitley Committee
principles effectively restructured collective bargaining across the
whole of the British economy outside the engineering and shipbuilding industries, and in Germany the collapse of the monarchy
led to a republican government that secured legal rights for national

collective bargaining and work-place employee representation. The period following the passage of the National Industrial Recovery Act in the United States, through to the end of the Second World War, transformed the pattern of American collective bargaining and trade unionism. In Sweden, the election of the first Social Democratic government in 1932 leading to the Saltsjobaden Agreement six years later, established principles of reciprocal relationships that were elaborated over the following decade, and then served as the model for the long postwar boom period ending in the early 1970s.

Two simple propositions can be advanced relating to these key periods of institutional development. First, they are essentially periods of acute sociopolitical change, which emerge from, and reflect, the pre-existing power resources available to the three main parties involved – state, employers and workers – and the outcome of which is decided by the interplay of those power resources. Second, the institutional and attitudinal arrangements which emerge out of these periods of accelerated change impose key constraints on the subsequent development of union organization and collective bargaining; they involve paradigm shifts.

The implication of the first proposition is that while economic factors such as inflation and unemployment may play an important role in the generation of crisis periods, their resolution will be decided by the interplay of the collective power of organizations, classes and ruling groups, rather than by purely economic processes. Econometric analysis may be able to point to reasons for the crisis, but cannot reasonably be expected to account for the outcomes, nor for the character of the 'paradigm' that results. Sociological and historical approaches to explanation may have equal difficulty with accurate prediction but are likely to offer more appropriate tools of analysis for the exploration of outcomes. Some brief examples of these critical periods of institutional development were given above. At the risk of over-simplification, and borrowing liberally from the recent work of another Warwick colleague Keith Sisson, I can propose a number of 'instances' or 'moments' of institutional development that have occurred in the key industrial nations.

Across continental Europe prior to the First World War there was very little formal accommodation between employers and trade unions, and the union movements were strongly politicized. The postwar crisis years of 1918–20 produced industry-wide multi-employer bargaining institutions in very many countries; underpinned to varying degrees by legislative regulation, these arrangements were designed to exclude unions from the work place while institutionalizing the power of organized labour at the national and industrial levels (Sisson 1987: 138–69; Sorge 1976: 283–5). In the United Kingdom, the latter part of the nineteenth century saw a long drawn-out battle between strong craft unions and the employers' associations in the key engineering and shipbuilding industries; this came to a head in the lock-out of 1898, and the settlement established the key procedural arrangements for the handling of work-place relationships for the following 70 years. The other key institutional break in Britain occurred at the end of the First World War with the implementation of joint industrial councils, and parallel 'Whitley' machinery in most of the public sector (Sisson 1987: 162–7). In the United States, the success of the 'open shop' campaign by the large corporations that were already dominating large sections of the US economy in the early years of the century meant that the craft unions of the American Federation of Labour (AFL) were not able to expand their membership base, 'remaining the preserve of highly-skilled, highly-paid craft workers employed mostly in the smaller establishments' (Sisson 1987: 177). This model of union organization and collective bargaining was dominant until the emergence from the depression brought both an internal political challenge to the AFL in the shape of the Congress of Industrial Organizations (CIO), and external political support via the National Recovery Act and the Wagner Act.

The importance of these 'paradigm breaks' is that they set the context for the period up to the next break – which may, of course, be a long time coming. The tightness of the constraints imposed by any particular 'settlement' is clearly variable. For instance, the elaborate legal code which the Weimar Republic imposed on collective bargaining, arbitration and work-place representation, provided an important underpinning for the maintenance of union organization throughout the period up to 1933, while the very much weaker French code was much less effective in its support of union organization. The comparison between France and Germany is instructive in another respect; while German union organization was dense and backed up, particularly in the populous industrial areas, by a network of party political, social and educational institutions, such institutional support was to be found very rarely in France (Berghahn & Karsten 1987: 144).

The 'shape' of any settlement comprises a range of 'external' elements such as the law, collective bargaining structures, the policy stances of key employers and their organizations, and the powers and role accorded to state regulatory bodies; and a wide range of 'internal' elements such as union structures, union organization, and political affiliations and ideological divisions in the ranks of organized labour. While it would be clearly incorrect to suggest that these key elements of the framework of relationships remain fixed throughout any 'paradigm period', the argument here is that within such periods any changes are ones of degree rather than of type. In the United Kingdom, for example, employers' attitudes became a good deal less accommodative once the crisis period at the end of the First World War was past, and many joint industrial councils fell into a semi-dormant state. Nevertheless, the structures remained largely intact, the legal system remained broadly unchanged, and even in the wake of the unions' defeat in the General Strike, victimization of individual union members did not extend to a wholesale destruction of the movement. In short, such variations as do occur do not alter the basic parameters of the system.

Within these periods of relative stability or institutional con-solidation, it seems reasonable to assume that, while economic, demographic and sociopolitical factors may all play some part in influencing the course of membership development, economic variables are likely to be more influential in such periods than in the periods of paradigm change – particularly in those countries where unions have an essentially economistic character. It is not surprising, therefore, to find that econometric analyses produce relatively high correlations between membership changes and the key labour market indicators, in countries like the United Kingdom, Australia, Canada, and the United States. It is equally unsurprising that economic variables are much less satisfactory in the explanation of membership developments in France, West Germany, Belgium, or Spain, since the framework within which the industrial relations system is operating during each 'consolidation' period is more heavily constrained by legal, institutional and political factors. In France, for example, the weakness of the collective bargaining system and of the unions' organizational infrastructure, together with the divisions within the union movement, dampen the impact of economic fluctuations on union membership very substantially. In every country, the impact of demographic and industrial or occupational change will have an independent effect on membership trends; in some periods, it may be so strong as to 'mask' the operation of other influences. The example of the United Kingdom, between 1980 and 1982, is an obvious one to cite here; membership plummeted by 1.7 million as unemployment in the heavily unionized manufacturing sector soared. While increased unemployment could be expected to reduce membership, its concentrated incidence in this one sector resulted in a disproportionate effect on aggregate membership levels.

This approach to analysis suggests, therefore, that periods of institutional consolidation will be characterized by relatively stable patterns of influence on the trajectory of union membership in any individual country. There may be a high degree of similarity between some countries giving rise to 'clusters' or 'families' of patterns of influence. But, while the same sets of factors may be present, it is *a priori* not probable that they will be weighted similarly – even within the clusters – since the institutional and sociopolitical frameworks established in the key periods of development differ so widely. To take some examples: Bain & Elsheikh found that membership changes in Australia were not significantly affected by price movements, unlike in the United Kingdom and the United States, because of the wage indexation element built into the arbitration system (Bain & Elsheikh 1976). Visser has noted that union membership has tended to increase in Belgium and Denmark as unemployment has risen, due very probably to the role played by unions in those countries in the administration of unemployment benefits (Visser 1987). In Sweden, the very high levels of union membership across all occupational groups, and the integration of the union confederations into the political and economic administration of the country, have largely insulated the course of union membership from year-on-year fluctuations in economic performance and political circumstances; membership figures show great stability. Many more examples could be cited, but the central point of this element of analysis is, hopefully, clear: the framework of union recognition, state and employer policies, and union organization set down during the periods of institutional development will condition the impact of any subsequent changes, whether economic or sociopolitical.

Recent developments

The approach to the analysis of union growth suggested here offers a number of important benefits. First, it makes it possible to integrate the apparently contradictory messages derived from the time-series and cross-sectional analyses undertaken by the leading writers in the field. Second, it allows for significant differences between countries while remaining within the same general framework of analysis. And third, it links theories of union growth to theories of trade unionism – an apparently obvious link, but one that has rarely informed previous debates about union growth.

It also takes account of one of the most effective criticisms of theories of union growth that rely on essentially exogenous variables; that unions are far from being the passive recipients of increases and losses imposed upon them by external forces, but can and do act to shape the economic, political and industrial environment. Periods of institutional development may be directly precipitated by union activity, either acting alone or as part of a wider labour movement. The power of unions may play a major or decisive role in the course of the period of development; the character and organization of the labour movement may exercise considerable influence over its ability to take advantage of favourable conjunctures for subsequent growth during consolidation periods – Visser, for example, argues that unified union systems lead to higher levels of unionization (1987: 151), while Kjellberg focuses on the combination of centralized and decentralized structures of representation as the key to high unionization rates (1983). The essential point is that institutional choices are made by unions when new 'paradigms' are being established, that may have continuing influence on their capacity to unionize. In one sense, this is Clegg's theoretical position approached from a different angle; instead of correlating bargaining depth with high density rates, union choices about bargaining activity are accepted as influences upon their capacity to recruit.

It is, however, an approach which lacks the appeal of a straight-forward three-variable model which can claim to explain Y per cent of the variance in country X, and A per cent in country B. In particular, the distinction between periods of institutional development and consolidation is imprecise and must run into some difficulty with periods of important, but not fundamental, change in the institutional framework – France under the Mauroy government, Britain in the social contract period, for example. Are these paradigm changes, or simply examples of sociopolitical 'tweaks' to an existing framework? This type of period is, in most cases, not fundamental enough to amount to a system change, and hence is best interpreted within the general analytical framework that has been used for the surrounding periods. Paradigm changes are rare.

A more general response to the criticism that this approach lacks precision is that, for the analysis of a social phenomenon that lies at the crossroads of economic, political, sociocultural and industrial influences, it is unlikely it could be otherwise if it is to provide satisfactory explanations. In the spirit of Weber's *verstehende Soziologie*, the scholar is called upon to use his or her judgement in interpreting the course of events in any individual society, but the approach does provide clear guidelines as to the type of factors that are likely to be influential in particular periods. A brief review of the evolution of union membership and density in the industrialized countries for which consistent data are available, from 1970 to 1985, may be helpful to illustrate the point.

This 16-year period was one of unusual turbulence and change in respect of all the key variables discussed earlier: structural changes in the labour force, economic factors, political factors, and employer policies. It can be divided into two contrasting sub-periods of roughly equal length: 1970–7, and 1978–85. The earlier sub-period was characterized by a mood of worker militancy and self-confidence that had its roots in the events of the latter half of the 1960s. During these years, price inflation was at historically high levels, and wages tended to follow suit. The first oil shock and the abolition of the Bretton Woods foreign exchange regime led to major changes in world trade patterns and stimulated decisive shifts in the domestic economic policies of many OECD countries – usually away from Keynesian demand management towards some form of monetarist system. The industrial turbulence of these years frequently induced governments to set up or reinforce tripartite and other 'corporatist' arrangements for economic management and to strengthen institutions for 'industrial democracy' and the humanization of work. Both these streams of political intervention reflected the concern of employers and the state to absorb worker 'militancy' by more effective integration of workers and their representatives into the machinery of state and enterprise decision-making. These economic and political trends were generally favourable to the growth of union membership. Inflation and wage movements were relatively high, stimulating the 'threat' and 'credit' effects identified by Bain & Elsheikh. Employer and state policies were favourable, seeking to accommodate worker demands and union pressures through positive changes in law and social policy. Unemployment rose above the low levels of the 1960s, but not by a large enough margin to affect union membership. Negative structural changes were occurring, particularly the shift away from manual towards non-manual work, but not on a large enough scale to counter the influences being felt from political and economic factors.

Table 4.2 illustrates these trends; large increases in aggregate union membership were recorded in the majority of industrialized countries between 1970 and 1977, and in no country did membership decline. After adjusting the aggregate data for labour force growth, 5 of the countries in the table experienced declines in density (Austria, France, Japan, Norway, and the United States), and the other 11 showed moderate to large increases. While the general movement of the economic indicators was favourable to union growth, the widely differing experiences among these countries reflect the heavily mediated impact of economic factors – mediated by the institutional and political environments established over long periods of institutional development.

Table 4.2   Changes in union membership and density levels – OECD countries 1970–1985.

	1970–7		1978–85	
	% Increase in union member- ship	Increase in density (% points)	% Increase in union member- ship	Increase in density (% points)
Australia	+20.6	+ 3.8 (1976)	+13.7	+ 0.3
Austria	+ 6.5	− 4	+ 2.7	+ 0.4 (1984)
Belgium	+ 7.2	+ 2 (1978)	+22.7	+ 6.7
Denmark	+28.0	+ 8.9	+20.1	+ 5.0*
France	+ 7.8	− 0.9	− 8.7*	− 3.2*
Germany, West	+10.9	+ 2.2	− 0.4	− 3.4
Ireland	+15.2	+ 1.3	− 3.5	− 8.9
Italy	+49.6	+ 9.4	− 2.4	− 4.2
Japan	+ 7.2	− 2.2	+ 0.3	− 3.7
Netherlands	+12.6	+ 1.6	−14.2	−10.0
New Zealand	+25.1	+ 3.8	+ 0.8	− 3.6
Norway	+16.5	− 1.2	+ 8.0	+ 5.1*
Sweden	+31.5	+12.5	+10.0	+ 2.3
Switzerland	+12.8	+ 5.5	− 2.2	− 1.8
United Kingdom	+14.8	+ 4.9	−18.3	−10.8
United States (Troy)	+ 3.0	− 3.4	−15.9	− 5.4 (1984)
(BLS)	+ 7.3	− 3.4 (1978)	−25.5	− 8.1

* Estimates

By contrast, the later sub-period shows only 5 countries with substantial increases in membership, 4 where membership was stable, and 7 where there were significant declines. In terms of union density levels, the contrast with 1970–7 is even more marked. There were significant increases in only 4 countries (Belgium, Norway, Sweden and Denmark), and major declines in several, particularly in the United States, the United Kingdom and the Netherlands. This reversal of the trends of the early 1970s is closely associated with the onset of world recession and increases in unemployment, particularly following the 1979 oil shock. At the same time, employers were adjusting to the competitive implications of micro-electronic technologies for both product design and manufacturing systems. While unemployment rose to levels that were well above the postwar average in most OECD countries, the degree to which individual countries suffered varied widely. But as in the earlier 'upturn' period the wide variation in individual countries' union growth experience cannot be ascribed uniquely to the variations in economic conditions; the impact of increased unemployment and new technologies was mediated by the varying 'paradigms' of institutions and expectations that had grown up in earlier periods.

The most direct effect of unemployment on union growth is to exclude from membership most employees who lose jobs in a unionized sector, and who either remain unemployed or find new jobs in a non-unionized environment. In the 4 countries where membership and density continued to increase after 1978, unions are involved in different ways in the administration of social security benefits and in job-search and training functions. The actual levels of unemployment experienced by this group of 4 varied widely, but in every case unions were able to offer continued benefits to former members, and to attract new members from amongst the unemployed, because of their role within the bipartite or tripartite machinery of social security provision. This rationale for continued membership attachment is absent in the majority of countries where the services offered by unions to the unemployed are negligible. In the case of Sweden, job-retraining facilities are provided on a scale which largely results in unemployed workers experiencing very short periods of non-participation in the labour force, thus further reducing the scope for dropping out of union membership.

Thus, in explaining the maintenance and growth of union membership in this group of countries, the structure of collective provision for retraining and income support is a key factor. It is a factor that is likely to be linked closely with a range of other structural relationships between state, employers and union, which exercise a critically important mediating role in determining the actual impact of unemployment upon the course of union membership. The relationship between the sectoral and occupational incidence of unemployment, and the distribution of union membership is also a key factor in determining the direct effect of unemployment on membership levels. In the United States and the United Kingdom, unemployment in the later period was disproportionately fuelled by the collapse of the heavily unionized 'smokestack' parts of the manufacturing sector. Similar, but less pronounced, sectoral reductions in employment have affected union membership levels in France, Ireland and the Netherlands. In West Germany, by contrast, the increase in unemployment has not been associated with cuts in manufacturing employment on anything like the same scale as elsewhere, and this has muted the direct impact of unemployment on membership.

More indirect effects of unemployment on union membership levels occur through the consequential reduction in perceived levels of union power. This can reduce the attractiveness of joining a union for current non-members, and it can provide the opportunity for employers and the state to press forward with policies that are designed to weaken union standing and effectiveness and, hence, ultimately, membership levels. In extreme cases, this latter type of offensive can so alter the terms of the relationship between capital and labour that a paradigm shift of the type discussed earlier takes place. It is arguably the case that this is what has been occurring in the United States and the United Kingdom during the extended depression of the early 1980s. In the United States, the so-called 'new industrial relations', involving concession bargaining, the drive to union-free work-places, government deregulation, and anti-union human resources policies, have strongly accentuated the negative membership trends that were already evident in the 1970s deriving mainly from occupational and geographical shifts in employment (Miller 1987). In the United Kingdom, the Thatcher administrations have rejected the 60-year cross-party consensus on the value of collective organization and collective representation. Unions have been excluded from a wide range of national consultative forums, and their representative role across wide swathes of public life has been substantially reduced. Legislative changes have severely undermined union security and reduced union capacity to undertake effective industrial action. Employers have been pursuing policies which, while not generally undermining union positions, have clearly cut back both their capacity for extension into new areas of membership and the impact of bargaining and consultative procedures. That the attempt to de-unionize the economy should have been most strongly pursued in these countries is clearly linked to the ideological position of their governments; that they should have been able to carry the policy through reflects important elements in the pre-existing frameworks of industrial relations in the two countries. Their conflictual orientation, as distinct from the 'social partnership' approach of the German or Austrian system; the absence of a strong and successful party–union relationship as in Sweden or Denmark; plant-based bargaining as opposed to multi-employer bargaining all make it easier to 'roll-up' recognition, and gradually reduce the scope of union influence. These are all distinctive factors which can be argued to have increased either the capacity of the state to press through an ideological offensive against collective employee representation, or the perceived advantages to be gained from doing so.

Concluding remarks

This chapter reflects the consensus that seems to have developed in the 1980s amongst union growth theorists in favour of combining 'structural' and 'cyclical' elements (Visser 1987: 150) or 'quantitative' and 'qualitative' approaches (Stepina & Fiorito 1986: 248). The long-term research at Warwick on the course of union growth and decline in the United Kingdom (e.g. Bain & Price 1983), deploys both long-term structural and short-term cyclical economic variables derived from earlier contributions to the theoretical debate with which we had been associated. This chapter seeks, in an inevitably schematic form, to offer a general approach to the analysis of union membership trends that can explain both time trends and inter-country variations and can combine both cross-sectional and longitudinal perspectives on the growth phenomenon.

The approach proposed here takes as its *point de départ* the small number of critical periods of institutional upheaval and renewal which are the key to the creation of 'systems' of institutions and patterns of reciprocal relationships. These periods have to be analysed 'qualitatively' and the principal actors are invariably the state, employers and the labour movement. During the relatively lengthy ensuing periods of institutional consolidation, when changes are incremental or insignificant, the balance of advantage in analysis shifts towards economic variables which will explain a large part – but certainly not all – of year-to-year variations. However, even granted the greater weight to be attached to economic variables in periods when the 'paradigm' or framework is changing only slightly, it should not be forgotten that the 20–30 per cent of variation not explained by economic variables can add up over the medium term to wide margins of inter-country variation. This points clearly to the importance of weaving an analytical cloth from both threads of influence. For European unions, the message from this analytical approach is probably rather unpalatable. With the exception of the Scandinavian countries, the current frameworks for union organization and bargaining do not favour the extension of membership into the new areas of employment growth. In the absence of a paradigm break, such as, for example, a pan-European legal initiative by the Commission of the European Communities, or a major social and political crisis, there seems little prospect of unions ending the century on an upbeat note.

References

This chapter is based on research undertaken by the author and several colleagues at the Industrial Relations Research Unit, University of Warwick. It draws in particular on valuable discussions and debates over the years with Professor George Bain and Professor Keith Sisson, and their contributions to the arguments developed here are gratefully acknowledged.

Ashenfelter, O. and J. H. Pencavel 1969. American trade union growth: 1900–1960. *Quarterly Journal of Economics* **LXXXIII**, August, 434–48.
Bain, G. S. 1970. *The Growth of White-Collar Unionism*. Oxford: Clarendon.
Bain, G. S. (ed.) 1983. *Industrial Relations in Britain*. Oxford: Blackwell.
Bain, G. S. & F. Elsheikh 1976. *Union Growth and the Business Cycle: An Econometric Analysis*. Oxford: Blackwell.
Bain, G. S. & R. Price 1983. Union growth: dimensions, determinants and destiny. In *Industrial Relations in Britain*, G. S. Bain (ed.), 3–33. Oxford: Blackwell.
Berghahn, V. & D. Karsten 1987. *Industrial Relations in West Germany*. Oxford: Berg.
Bernstein, I. 1954. The growth of American unions. *American Economic Review* **XLIV**, June, 301–18.

Clegg, H. A. 1976. *Trade Unions Under Collective Bargaining*. Oxford: Blackwell.

Commons, John R. & associates 1918. *History of Labor in the United States*. Vol. 1. New York: Macmillan.

Davis, H. B. 1941. The theory of union growth. *Quarterly Journal of Economics* **LV**, August, 611–37.

Dunlop, J. T. 1948. The development of labor organization: a theoretical framework. In *Insights into Labor Issues*, R. A. Lester, & J. Shister (eds), 163–93. New York: Macmillan.

Flanders, A. 1970. What are unions for? In *Management and Unions*, A. Flanders (ed.), 38–47. London: Faber.

Hines, A. G. 1964. Trade unions and wage inflation in the United Kingdom, 1893–1961. *Review of Economic Studies* **XXXI**, October, 221–50.

Kjellberg, A. 1983. *Facklig Organisering i tolv länder*. Lund.

Miller, R. 1987. The mid-life crisis of the American labor movement. *Industrial Relations Journal* **18**, 3, 159–69.

Sisson, K. 1987. *The Management of Collective Bargaining: An International Comparison*. Oxford: Blackwell.

Sorge, A. 1976. The evolution of industrial democracy in the countries of the European Community. *British Journal of Industrial Relations* **XIV**, 3, 274–94.

Stepina, L. P. & J. Fiorito 1986. Towards a comprehensive theory of union growth and decline. *Industrial Relations* **25**, 3, 248–64.

Visser, J. 1987. *In Search of Inclusive Unionism: A Comparative Analysis*. Amsterdam.

Visser, J. 1988. Trade unionism in Western Europe: present situation and prospects. *Labour and Society* **13**, 2, 125–82.

Webb, S. & B. Webb 1894. *The History of Trade Unionism*. London: Longman.

5 *Management and industrial relations*

D. H. PLOWMAN

There is a growing awareness of the need to incorporate the role of management in the study of labour relations. This chapter examines attempts to conceptualize and research management, both as a collective and an individual entity, with respect to labour. To a large extent the collective entity is defined by the external or institutionalized functions of employer associations. The individual entity is defined by the functions of management within the enterprise or corporation. The first section of the chapter deals with the collective entity, the second with management strategies and control.

The collective entity: employer associations

Though there continues to be a relative paucity of theorizing into employer associations, there has been a growth in literature on the collective activities of employers (Plowman 1987). Typically, this literature depicts associations as reactive institutions which have come into being to protect members from the activities of either unions or the state or both. Associations have sought to regulate trade and competition, to provide a united front in negotiations, and to provide a range of services. Employers combine on the basis of their trade, a source of inter-association conflict. In many countries, there has been an evolution from evanescent, to belligerent, and then to negotiatory associations as employers have come to terms with unions.

As well as detailing a host of other minutiae concerning employer association structures and organization, the literature suggests three major areas of concern which this chapter will examine: the role of employer associations in determining bargaining structures; the determinants of single- and multi-employer bargaining; and frameworks for conceptualizing employer associations.

Since the publication of the Webbs' *Industrial Democracy* (1897), collective bargaining has been regarded as a union method of regulation. This view has increasingly come under challenge and there is now a body of literature which postulates that employer associations have not only been favourably disposed towards collective bargaining, but were also its instigators.

Employers' favourable disposition towards collective (multi-employer) bargaining is the product of several factors. Collective bargaining helps prevent unions from whip-sawing between companies. It places a floor under wages and takes them out of competition. Collective bargaining helps provide both managerial and market controls. It assists in the avoidance of costly strikes, and where these cannot be avoided employers have reasonable expectations that they will not result in any permanent loss of market share. Managerial prerogatives are preserved under collective bargaining (Clegg 1979, Flanders 1974, Fox 1975, Phelps Brown 1959).

The contention that employers were the initiators of collective bargaining is most evident in the writings of Clegg and, through him, the United Kingdom's Royal Commission on Trade Unions and Employers' Associations (the Donovan Commission). The latter claimed employer associations to be the 'innovators' in collective bargaining. They instituted collective bargaining in industries such as coal and iron, before stable unions were formed. In many industries, including the iron and hosiery industries, they took the initiative in developing collective bargaining on a district basis. In 'important industries', including engineering and building, the employers' associations forced the unions, in some instances through prolonged lock-outs, to accept the first principle of industry-wide bargaining – that local disputes should be submitted to a central conference 'before a strike or lock-out is begun' (*Report of Royal Commission on Trade Unions and Employers' Associations* 1967: 20–1).

Clegg has taken this analysis further and argues the case that employers and their associations ought to be regarded as the major determinants of bargaining structures, in short that collective bargaining is an employer, rather than a union method of regulation. In his book *Trade Unionism under Collective Bargaining* (1976), he develops the theory that differences in union behaviour can be explained by differences in collective bargaining. In addition to the state 'if it comes in at a sufficiently early stage', Clegg sees the structure and attitudes of employer associations and management as the main direct influences upon collective bargaining (p. 10).

In a later work Clegg has applied his thesis to the British situation and demonstrates that employers have been influential in establishing centralized procedural and substantive rules (Clegg 1979: 62–70).

A similar analysis has been applied on a more global basis by Adams (1981) and Sisson (1986). The former provides what might be called the 'neutralizing thesis' to explain why European employers have been more prepared to deal with unions than their North American counterparts. He writes that the socialist, mass-based European unions at the turn of the century caused governments to force union recognition on employers. Employers acceded to government pressures rather than run the gauntlet of more intrusive government interference. However, having been forced to recognize unions, employers took the initiative to neutralize their socialist objectives at the enterprise by forcing them to recognize management's rights as a quid pro quo for their own recognition, and by removing bargaining away from the enterprise to the industry level. In some cases, employers were also successful in forcing a restructuring of craft unions into industry unions. In this analysis, the lack of mass-based unions in the United States, and the economic rather than political orientation of these unions, resulted in no serious threat to capitalism. As a result, governments did not force union recognition upon employers.

Sisson's work, and what might be termed his 'historic compromise thesis', also sees the political orientation of European unions as an important element in shaping the origins of collective bargaining. Importantly, however, he also explores why it is that in different situations employers have chosen to recognize unions either by way of multi-employer or by single-employer bargaining. He concludes that bargaining structures 'are not the result of individual employers and trade unions or, for that matter, governments making rational choices from a range of possible options'. Nor does Sisson consider bargaining structures to be the reflection of any evolutionary process. He argues instead that they are rooted in specific compromises involving many employers.

For governments the institutionalization of industrial conflict was usually an end in itself. For employers, however, it was a means to an end: the maintenance of managerial control, in particular the legitimacy that union involvement in the rule-making process gave to the employers' right to manage.

To understand why the main dimensions of bargaining emerged in the way they did, it is necessary to 'appreciate the relationship between employers and trade unions at the time the compromise was made'. In the European context of socialist unions multi-employer bargaining was advantageous to employers. It reinforced non-wage competition, enabled employers to meet trade union demands with a single act of recognition, maximized employers' bargaining power, and made it possible for employers to neutralize the work place from trade union activity.

In the United States and Japan large employers emerged at a relatively early stage of industrialization. Unions were suppressed for a long period. In those countries single-employer bargaining appeared the lesser of two evils. Companies did not have to unscramble their own internal systems of job regulation, which also served to neutralize unions' work-place activities.

Sisson's analysis is a useful one for giving the general framework for single- and multi-employer bargaining. His rather broad-brush treatment does disguise some of the diversity which exists in both predominantly single-employer and multi-employer contexts, but these can be readily incorporated using Sisson's own rationale. In the context of multi-employer bargaining, for example, it has been noted that large companies often refrain from joining the relevant employer associations (e.g. Dufty 1984: 129). Conversely, in the American context, in which the Sisson schema is one of single-employer bargaining, multi-employer bargaining is a feature of those industries not dominated by corporate giants (Derber 1984, Carpenter 1950, Slate 1957, Munson 1962).

The general lack of systematic study of employer associations has meant that there are few established frameworks for analysing these institutions. One approach has been to adapt labour movement theories to the study of employer associations (Plowman 1983). In one such theory, that of the extension of the market, John Commons (1909) provides as much a theory of employer associations as of unions. Since Commons's theory is well known, it will not be detailed in this chapter. Rather, this section will examine three recent attempts to conceptualize employer associations: McCaffree's 'adaptive' theory, the three-model approach of Jackson & Sisson, and the corporatist framework of Streeck.

On the basis of his study of the Associated Industries of the Inland Empire, McCaffree (1962: 57) has attempted to develop a theory of the origins and development of associations. His 'central thesis is the proposition that local employer associations... arise exogenously and are purely responsive and adaptive in their development. Factors in the environment of the employer and not his endogenous interests in the labour market "cause" the formation of the associations. As those factors change, so will the nature and activities of the employer organization.'

McCaffree claims three elements to be crucial to the explanation of the origins and growth of employer associations: unions, government agencies, and trade associations, with the latter being greatly influenced by product technology. These factors are 'environmental and exogenous to the firm'. McCaffree considers, but dismisses, monopsony as an inducement to organization. He notes that the 'overwhelming impression... is the dominant role of unions and unionism in the origin and development of this association... The principle is clear enough: employers band together in response to the external threats of unionism. The association is a defense against unions. Employers, through the association, can prevent unions from using whip-saw tactics successfully against them. Nor can the direct threat to the traditional managerial prerogatives be overlooked' (1962: 62).

The second 'environmental factor', government agencies, has been important because of the way the National Labor Relations Act, the National Labor Relations Board (NLRB) and the National War Labor Board facilitated employer organization. McCaffree notes the influence of employer groups on wages determined under NLRB regulations 'and the advantages of co-operation under such circumstances' (1962: 64). Further, early interpretations of the Wagner Act by the NLRB, which favoured industrial unions over the craft union, encouraged industry-wide bargaining units and the formation of employer groups to conduct such negotiations.

The trade association, which is built around product markets and along industry lines, is important in three respects: product market associations have been converted to handle labour problems; the product orientation of associations demonstrates the essential community of interest of an association; the product market highlights the effects and importance of new products and new methods on existing organizations and upon the formation of new associations.

Jackson & Sisson (1975) propose a three-model approach to the study of employer associations. The first of these is the defensive model in which employers combine against unions. The objectives of these defensive associations are very limited: 'protecting employers from the encroachment of trade unions'. Though it 'offers a fairly accurate description of the events which led to the formation of employers' organizations in many cases', they recognize that 'this model leaves many questions unanswered'. They conclude that the model 'might explain why an employers' organization was formed, but it does not explain why collective bargaining subsequently developed. Strictly speaking, then, it is questionable whether the traditional or defensive model is a model at all' (p. 6).

The second model is the procedural or political model. Employer associations may develop in response to unions, but much greater significance is to be attached to the events which follow. Employers accept unions and collective bargaining over the basic terms and conditions of employment as a quid pro quo for unions accepting employers' right to manage and for the establishment of orderly grievance procedures. The emphasis, in this case, is on the institutionalization of conflict. As with the defensive model, the procedural model 'appears to fit the facts in many instances'. It is also 'fundamental in its implications, since the responsibility for determining the scope as well as the level of collective bargaining is attributed to employers' (p. 6). However, like the defensive model it does not adequately explain some of the differences in management behaviour or the levels at which collective bargaining takes place. Further, a number of employer associations cannot be explained in terms of the procedural model.

The third model is the market or economic model. It attributes the responsibility for determining the scope of bargaining to employers but also suggests the factors which may result in the levels of bargaining which occur. Critical to this model is the observation that employers tend to organize and co-operate along product lines. Thus, organization against unions is only one consideration. The market model 'yields a number of significant propositions which can at least be tested in empirical research... but like the other models, it is not without its weakness'. The powers of prediction of this model 'seem much weaker in the case of the less intensively competitive industries than the competitive ones' (p. 8). Further, contrary to this model's assumptions, there is evidence of large companies playing a major part in the formation and development of employer associations in many countries.

Jackson & Sisson conclude that, between them, 'the three models or variants of them would appear to supply most of the underlying variables which help to explain the nature and extent of employer organization' (p. 8).

Influenced by his studies of business associations in West Germany, Wolfgang Streeck (1982) has hypothesized that the pluralist paradigm underpinning most approaches to the study of employer associations is in need of re-evaluation and that a corporatist framework may provide a better explanation of the operations and development of employer associations. Though employer associations may have started out as pluralist 'state-free' organizations, they have been 'drawn by the state into neo-corporatist structures of collective discipline and responsibility' (p. 5). This corporatist involvement has emerged in an incremental manner in which expediency, rather than any coherent ideology, has been to the fore. Streeck remarks on the 'continuous character' of the relations between established peak associations and the state. This is explained, in part, by the tendency of the modern state 'to intervene in all spheres of social and economic life, and its time-consuming rituals of participation, public debates and consensus building'. Integration is also the result of organizational considerations. Recognition and support by the state improve an organization's political influence and membership prospects, an important consideration for peak organizations. Such recognition also assists the state since 'by helping sustain a unified and centralized interest associational structure, the State reduces the complexity of the demands made upon its decisions, and it acquires a capacity to make demands on associational resources and policies in return'. Another organizational imperative is the desire of employer bodies to seek self-regulation in preference to state regulation. The desire to self-regulate so as to pre-empt state intervention, however, weakens the bargaining power of associations in relation to the state. Further the state can offload regulatory functions to associations and 'realize its political objectives without having to take upon itself the risks and burdens of implementing them on its own'. This process may transform associations into *de facto* state agencies.

Since there has been little general application of these frameworks there is scant empirical evidence by which to assess their usefulness. On the basis of my study of national employer co-ordination in Australia over the period 1890–1980 I would make the following observations. I did not find the Commons schema, or that of Streeck, fitted the general contours of the Australian experience, though the latter may have increasing relevance in the future. Surprisingly, in view of its breadth, neither did the Jackson & Sisson three-model approach provide a particularly useful framework for explaining the Australian experience (Plowman 1988). McCaffree's 'adaptive' model proved the best explanation. However, the Australian study suggested desirable modifications to the 'adaptive' model. Thus, though the external environment may well trigger adaptive responses as McCaffree suggests, his model does not appear capable of predicting the nature or timing of those responses. It does not explain, for example, why some trade associations responded to changed circumstances by diversifying to become employer associations while others chose to remain trade associations which affiliated in employers' federations. Further, the history of national employer co-ordination in Australia would suggest that though exogenous factors provide the necessary conditions under which associations are forced to adapt, endogenous factors are important determinants of the nature of that change. Once associations are formed they take on an identity which helps define an endogenous organizational context. Thus the appropriate framework for the study of employer associations would appear to be one which gives attention to both the exogenous environmental factors and internal or endogenous factors. The latter include the calibre, dynamism and personalities of association leaders; membership composition; internal authority structures; the recruitment catchment areas; the range of areas to which the association has to devote its attention; internal stability; financial and other resources; and inter-organizational relationships.

The manager: strategy and control

Space does not permit a full review of the burgeoning literature on the management of industrial relations. Rather, this section will focus on two interrelated aspects of this literature: managerial frames of reference and strategic management. The latter incorporates not only aspects of management control (including the labour process literature) but also neo-institutionalist approaches to industrial relations.

Managerial frames of reference were given vogue by Alan Fox's (1966) contribution to the UK Donovan Commission. In this he identified two major frames of reference: the unitarist and the pluralist. The former sees only one source of authority, and one focus of loyalty, within the enterprise. There is the vision of a 'team approach' with all members 'pulling in the same direction'. There are no oppositions or factions. There are common objectives and common values which unite and bind together all participants. Disputation is considered an aberration, abnormal and irrational. Unions are considered unnecessary and, at best, anachronistic.

The pluralist framework sees the enterprise as a coalition of individuals and groups with their own interests, agendas and power bases. There is some degree of collaboration in the social structure which enables all participants to get something of what they want. Management makes decisions within a complex set of constraints which includes not only employees, but also consumers, suppliers, governments, the law, financial institutions, shareholders and the local community. Management, like the other elements in the pluralist society, must compromise. The enterprise itself 'is seen as a complex of tensions and competing claims which have to be "managed"'. Management has to compete with other sources of leadership and other focuses of loyalty. It must share its decision-making. A corollary is that conflict is endemic, and a natural part of management–employee relations. Trade unions constitute one pressure group, and the compromises with this group are usually extracted through collective bargaining.

The pluralist ideology has been the source of much debate, much of it with the hidden agenda of seeking to demonstrate or refute Marxist analysis of the inevitability of class conflict. In this debate many writers have moved away from managerial frames of reference to attempts to explain or codify the industrial relations system (or indeed the total social system) within which management operates. This is true of Fox's (1974) subsequent work which introduces a third frame of reference – the radical perspective. This prescriptive (as opposed to descriptive) frame of reference shares much with Marxism.

In the view of one reviewer Fox's radical perspective 'represents a challenge to his former pluralistic colleagues which they cannot pass over in silence without a serious loss of intellectual credibility' (Goldthorpe 1975). Wood & Elliot (1977: 105) contend that Fox's radical view does not 'represent a fundamentally radical break from liberal-pluralism' but Fox (1979) has responded by claiming that they have misread and misrepresented his work. Clegg's (1975) criticism, and his articulation of the pluralists' paradigm, have not been countered. For Clegg the social fabric (and industrial relations systems) is held together by the 'continuous process of concession and compromise'. Pluralism exists where pressure groups have the freedom to operate and where their capacity to abuse power is constrained. Compromise is the norm, but, contrary to Fox's claim, is not inevitable. Since the values and principles guiding contesting parties are not derived from pluralism itself, compromises which clash too violently with the values of different causes will be rejected. Clegg also challenges and rejects Fox's contention that pluralism implies a balance of power between the various parties. Since Fox's rejection of pluralism is derived from the illusion of a balance of power, demolishing that illusion does no damage to pluralism. Neither does it lend support to a radical perspective.

A major attribute of the pluralist–radical debate has been the lack of clarification of the descriptive, normative and prescriptive aspects of the frameworks and embodied ideology. Though at the prescriptive level the radical and pluralist frameworks differ, at the descriptive level they share much in common (see Clegg 1979: 455–6).

The generality of Fox's frames of reference, and the mutually exclusive nature of these frameworks, limits their usefulness. They are of little help in themselves in drawing distinctions between the style or approach of managements in different organizations, many of which recognize unions and engage in collective bargaining. In *Beyond Contract*, Fox (1974) presents six ideal-type patterns of management–employee relations which allow for the amplification of the frames of reference. These are the traditional, classical conflict, sophisticated modern, standard modern, sophisticated paternalist, and continuous challenge patterns.

The traditional pattern is characterized by a unitary perspective on the part of both management and employees. 'Since management's prerogative is not even ideologically, still less practically, contested, its definition of roles and rewards is fully legitimized' (p. 297). Once employees' consciousness has been aroused, this pattern gives way to the classical conflict pattern. Unions and collective bargaining appear. Relations are conflictual, antagonistic and low trust.

Management, which may see positive benefits from collective bargaining, may move to the mutual accommodation or the sophisticated modern pattern. In this, both management and employees share the pluralistic ideology. Management legitimizes the union role in certain areas since this is conducive to its own interests. Purcell & Sisson (1983) subdivide this group into the 'constitutionalists' and the 'consultors'. For the first group the limits of collective bargaining are clearly codified by the collective agreement. The 'consultors' have no wish to codify everything in the agreement, and attempt to minimize conflictual or distributive bargaining.

The sophisticated modern pattern is regarded as highly unstable. 'It represents an equilibrium situation, and in a constantly changing world any equilibrium is uncertain and precarious.' It may revert back to the classical conflict pattern, but commonly it slides into the standard modern pattern. This pattern is characterized by ambivalence within management towards the pluralist ideology, an ambivalence of two forms. Some members of management will be convinced unitarians, others pluralists. Individual managers may fluctuate between these two positions according to circumstances. Unitarism is emphasized at times of crises and emergencies. At other times management's mixture of unitarism and pluralism leads to confusion and uncertainty. This pattern is labelled standard modern (management-divided). Since work groups of different occupations may divide along unitary and pluralist lines, another division is that of standard modern (employee-divided). Purcell (1983) has developed the strategic management implications of this pattern.

The sophisticated paternalist pattern is the combination of a wholly or partly pluralistic management and a predominantly unitary-minded labour force. Management, for one reason or another, finds itself dealing with a largely inert unionized workforce with little assertive leadership. Management deals directly with full-time union officers outside the plant and comes under no direct challenge from within the plant in its day-to-day control. The union hierarchy plays its role in regulating the terms and conditions of employment 'without being subject to complicating pressures and cross-currents from the regulated' (Fox 1974: 298).

The continuous challenge, or non-accommodative, pattern is similar to the classical conflict pattern but with a reversal of roles. Instead of management refusing to legitimize employees' claims, work groups refuse to legitimize management's claim to assert and pursue objectives which override the groups' interests. No systematic and stable pattern of mutual accommodation emerges and no equilibrium relationships develop; 'only periods of uneasy armed truce as each side licks its wounds and watches the enemy for signs of a weak spot in its defenses' (Fox 1974: 298). Clearly, this pattern has moved out of the pluralist into the radical perspective. These six patterns have enabled some analysis of management strategies (Fox 1974, Purcell 1983, Purcell & Sisson 1983).

In attempting to clarify the meaning of management style (the choices made by management and the underlying rationale), Purcell (1987) finds the need to go beyond some of the limitations of the frames of reference debate. Three major limitations are found to exist: the wide variations of conduct to be found within those subscribing to a unitarist or pluralistic perspective; the mutually exclusive nature of the frames of reference; and the lack of clarification as to whether the frames of reference apply to management's dealings with organized labour or individual employees.

Purcell notes that 'in practice, as well as theory, firms can have broad policies or guiding principles toward both the attention to be given to employees and their individual group needs, and in regard to trade unions and other types of collective labour organization. Such policies are not necessarily mutually exclusive' (1987: 536). Purcell suggests that these two dimensions of management style can be identified with individualism and collectivism.

Individualism refers to the extent to which firms develop and encourage each employee's capacity and role at work. Three types are noted: high individualism with its emphasis on employee development; low individualism with its concern with labour market control and a 'commodity' approach to labour; and paternalistic individualism, which represents something of a halfway house.

Collectivism refers to management's dealings with organized labour. Management may take a constitutionalist or a consultative approach to unions or other forms of employee representatives.

Under this division of management styles it is possible to identify a dual approach by management to labour relations: a unitarist approach towards individuals (and possible in-plant 'personnel' matters), and a pluralist approach towards unions and other 'externalities'.

The publication of Braverman's *Labor and Monopoly Capital* (1974) has given rise to a mass of labour process literature. Three major areas of concern have been de-skilling, the nature of labour markets, and managerial strategy and control. This chapter looks at the last of these concerns.

Labour process theory asserts that the ultimate function of management is the conversion of labour power (workers' potential) into actual labour under conditions which allow for capital accumulation

(Braverman 1974: chapter 1). Different phases of capitalism are seen to evoke different forms of managerial control. Braverman sees monopoly capitalism as entailing extensive job fragmentation and job specialization. The primary impetus behind job design is that of de-skilling. Job fragmentation and de-skilling are vehicles of job control.

The paradigm has come under much criticism (e.g. Friedman 1977, Wood 1982, Littler 1982, Storey 1983, Knights *et al.* 1985). One area of criticism has been the unilinear and deterministic nature of Braverman's schema. Researchers have not been able to find a clear link between different phases of capitalism and phases in the work process. This, in turn, has led to an interest in managerial strategy. If there is no iron law determining the nature of the labour process, perhaps events may be understood in terms of management strategies. Littler (1987) notes three lines of interrogation: the implications of rationality in the concept of managerial strategy; the relationship between strategy and implementation; and the extent to which the labour process is the main point of reference for managerial policy. The first two points are examined later since they are also relevant to the non-labour process literature which deals with management strategy.

The notion that the labour process is the central focus of managerial strategies is an alien one to those who see strategy in the Chandler tradition. In this tradition the development of modern corporations is explained by reference to long-term strategic investment rather than by consideration of labour issues. It suggests that labour control is not the central concern of capitalist management. Indeed, labour control may be peripheral. Thus, Littler & Salaman (1982) have noted that non-labour derived income plays a major role, perhaps the dominant role, in many enterprises – currency speculation, cumulative acquisitions and asset stripping, commodity speculation, credit manipulations, etc. They note: 'Surplus value has to be produced but also *realized* in the market. What this implies is that the realization of surplus value (i.e. finding markets, selling in those markets and making a profit) may be more crucial than the production of surplus value for certain firms, certain industries or during certain periods' (p. 63). Production management and labour control may not be the dominant management consideration. A prime consideration for the labour process paradigm is to determine the circumstances in which labour strategies dominate managerial initiatives.

Braverman's postulate of a linear process of de-skilling and control is bereft of any concept of managerial strategy. Edwards's *Contested Terrain* (1979) also assumes an essentially linear process and identifies three historical forms of control: simple, direct control; technological control; and bureaucratic control. These typologies are not dissimilar to the three basic types of managerial control identified by Woodward (1970). Edwards argues that direct control prevailed during the competitive period of capitalism and involved harsh and sometimes capricious treatment by owners and managers. Technological control determined the pace and content of work and was itself the product of plant layout and 'the imperatives of the production technology'. Worker resistance to this form of control, and the increasing size of organizations, led to a second type of structure-based strategy, bureaucratic control. This control is 'embedded in the social and organization structure of the firm, is built into job categories, work rules, promotion procedures, discipline, wage scales, definitions of responsibility, and the like' (p. 131). Edwards's historical process shares a common deficiency with that of Braverman: the evidence suggests no simple evolution of phases in the development of capitalism. Despite the rejection of Edwards's history, his categories have been utilized in a number of ways.

Friedman (1977), like others, is critical of the single implied managerial strategy of Braverman – the securing of managerial control. He argues that the corporation's goals can be achieved by different strategies. He refers to these as 'responsible autonomy' and 'direct control'. In the former, managers emphasize labour's positive features, particularly its malleability. Supervision is restricted, loyalty rewarded, and workers are granted responsibility and status and welfare facilities. There is co-operation with unions. Under direct control managers reduce worker autonomy and responsibility and increase the role of supervisors. These classifications can be easily subsumed into Fox's managerial frames. They also share much in common with McGregor's (1960) Theory X and Theory Y.

Burawoy (1979) also identifies two modes of control, despotic and hegemonic. Despotic control resembles Edwards's simple control or Friedman's direct control. Hegemonic control refers to a more sophisticated way of winning consent and has clear parallels with Edwards's 'bureaucratic control'. In a later work Burawoy (1983) has elaborated on these two types of managerial strategy and has added a third, that of hegemonic despotism. This ill-defined strategy seems to refer to the economic power arising from the mobility of capital and 'the fear of capital flight, plant closure, the transfer of operations, and disinvestment' (p. 603).

Another non-linear historic approach which encapsulates managerial control strategies is that of Gospel (1983a, 1983b). He is particularly concerned with the structure of labour management, which he defines as 'the various organizational forms and personnel which entrepreneurs have used to recruit and maintain a labour force; to monitor, discipline, and reward workers; and to deal with trade unions as they emerged' (1983a: 6). The major forms of labour management identified are the 'putting-out system', subcontracting, wage-earning foremen, central employment departments, and employer associations. Gospel argues that 'the growth of multi-unit enterprises has also been accompanied by strategic choices by management'. Some have adopted federal structures, others centralized structures. In Gospel's view the choice of structure has been determined by a number of factors such as the product range and the degree of autonomy in other areas of management. These factors might suggest that labour control has not been the paramount consideration. Thus, though one might agree with Gospel that the development of structural forms 'both reflected and facilitated changes in managerial strategies', it is less clear that structural forms have labour control as their principal goal. In short, structural form has been geared to the corporation's major goal – production and profitability – rather than to an element of that goal (labour management). Labour management has conformed to a given structural form, rather than determined that form.

Management strategy, or more aptly strategic management, is also an element in the pluralist literature. The work of Kochan *et al.* (1986) which, like Braverman's work, has an historical basis, provides a useful contrast with the more deterministic and selective features of the labour process paradigm.

Kochan *et al.* view the historic changes in the US industrial relations system as the product of environmental pressures and organizational strategies. Their central argument 'is that industrial relations practices and outcomes are shaped by the interactions of environmental forces along with the strategic choices and values of American managers, union leaders, workers and public policy decision-makers'. They place management values and strategies at the centre of their analysis of recent changes because 'since the 1960s union behaviour and government policy have been much slower than employers to adapt to changes in their external environment and to changes in managerial strategies and policies' (p. 9).

Without using the terms, they conclude that American managers have a unitarist frame of reference, even though public policy has been built around a pluralist framework – the notion of a legitimate conflict of interests in employment relations. They criticize Dunlop and other supporters of the systems approach which assume a shared ideology following New Deal legislation. 'The conclusion that management had adopted and accepted unions as legitimate partners', they write, 'misinterpreted as a change in managerial preferences or ideology what was actually a pragmatic or strategic adaptation to the high costs of avoiding or dislodging established unions' (p. 9). With environmental changes, managers were able to introduce the 'new industrial relations' which reflected a unitarist perspective.

Building on Chandler's work Kochan *et al.* develop a three-tiered strategic-choice institutional framework. This involves consideration of strategy at three levels: top management, collective bargaining cum personnel policy, and work place. The first of these is significant. Rather than merely focusing upon the role of the industrial relations function within a given management structure, it enables consideration of the strategies and 'events having significant impact on industrial relations processes and outcomes [which] start well above the functional level of industrial relations within the firm' (p. 10).

Kochan *et al.* use their strategic-choice model to analyse the historical development of US labour relations. While proving a useful model for ex-post analysis, it provides a less useful predictive model. 'Given the strategic-choice perspective developed', the authors note, 'we áre particularly unwilling to make predictions for the future based on projections of past trends' (p. 227). Instead the authors demonstrate the range of choices open to the parties. The final outcome will be the result of environmental pressures and the parties' strategies, rather than something which has been predetermined.

The strategic-choice model is useful for addressing two problem areas noted earlier: the implications of rationality in the concept of management strategy, and the relationship between intended strategy and implementation. The model also provides a means of tackling the empirical evidence suggesting a lack of labour relations strategy on the part of management.

A number of organizational studies have indicated what has been termed a 'fire brigade' approach to management. Management is caught up with day-to-day crises rather than working from long-term strategies. For those like Rose & Jones (1985) for whom strategy entails a degree of 'consciousness, rationality, permanency or fixity of purpose and a detailed plan or campaign broadly accepted across levels and segments of management' the organizational studies would suggest an absence of strategy (Littler 1987). The environmental pressures which form an important input in the strategic-choice model make it easy to agree with Littler that the Rose & Jones approach represents an over-rationalized concept of strategy. All choices are constrained and so long as these 'fall within a certain pattern we are entitled to talk about "management strategy"'.

The empirical evidence suggests that not only do organizations proceed on the basis of the fire brigade approach, but also that pragmatism and opportunism, rather than a strategic approach, are the hallmark of labour-management relations (e.g. Purcell & Ahlstrand 1988, Hegarty & Hoffman 1987). The strategic-choice model directs attention away from those levels generally examined in the industrial relations literature – the personnel and work levels – to a higher order. It also directs attention to the fact that industrial relations decisions often constitute second order choices which are deeply influenced by first order business policy considerations (Purcell & Ahlstrand 1988).

The strategic-choice model also highlights why intended strategy may not become realized strategy. Environmental factors, as well as the opposing and competing strategies of the other parties, result in 'leakages' between strategy formulation and achievement. They also result in the need for management constantly to reformulate its strategies.

References

Adams, R. J. 1981. A theory of employer attitudes and behaviour towards trade unions in Western Europe and North America. In *Management under Differing Value Systems*, G. Dlugos & K. Weiermair (eds), 277–93. New York: de Gruyter.

Braverman, H. 1974. *Labor and Monopoly Capital*. New York: Monthly Review Press.

Burawoy, M. 1979. *Manufacturing Consent*, Chicago: University of Chicago Press.

Burawoy, M. 1983. Between the labour process and the state: changing face of factory regimes under advanced capitalism. *American Sociological Review* **48**, October, 587–605.

Carpenter, J. 1950. *Employer Associations and Collective Bargaining in New York City*. Ithaca, NY: Cornell University Press.

Chandler, D. 1966. *Strategy and Structure*. New York: Anchor Books.

Clegg, H. 1975. Pluralism and industrial relations. *British Journal of Industrial Relations* **XIII**, 3, 309–16.

Clegg, H. 1976. *Trade Unionism under Collective Bargaining*. Oxford: Blackwell.

Clegg, H. 1976. *The Changing System of Industrial Relations in Great Britain*. Oxford: Blackwell.

Commons, J. 1909. American shoemakers 1648–1895. *Quarterly Journal of Economics* **XXIV**, November, 210–64.

Derber, M. 1984. Employer associations in the United States. In *Employers Associations and Industrial Relations: A Comparative Study*, J. P. Windmuller & A. Gladstone (eds), 79–114. Oxford: Clarendon.

Dufty, N. 1984. Employer associations in Australia. In *Employers Associations and Industrial Relations: A Comparative Study*, J. P. Windmuller & A. Gladstone (eds), 115–48. Oxford: Clarendon.

Edwards, R. 1979. *Contested Terrain*. London: Heinemann.

Flanders, A. 1974. The tradition of voluntarism. *British Journal of Industrial Relations* **XII**, 2, 352–70.

Fox, A. 1966. *Industrial Sociology and Industrial Relations*. Research Paper no. 3, Royal Commission on Employer Associations and Trade Unions. London: HMSO.

Fox, A. 1974. *Beyond Contract: Work, Power and Trust Relations*. London: Faber.

Fox, A. 1975. Collective bargaining, Flanders and the Webbs. *British Journal of Industrial Relations* **XIII**, 2, 151–74.

Fox, A. 1979. A note on industrial-relations pluralism. *Sociology* **13**, 105–9.

Friedman, A. 1977. *Industry and Labour*. London: Macmillan.

Goldthorpe, J. 1975. Review of A. Fox, *Beyond Contract*. In *British Journal of Industrial Relations* **XIII**, 1, 134–7.

Gospel, H. 1983a. Managerial structure and strategies: an introduction. In *Managerial Strategies and Industrial Relations*, H. F. Gospel & C.R. Littler (eds), 1–24. London: Heinemann.

Gospel, H. 1983b. The development of management organization in industrial relations: a historical perspective. In *Industrial Relations and Management Strategy*, K. Thurley & S. Wood (eds), 91–110. Cambridge: Cambridge University Press.

Hegarty, W. H. and R. G. Hoffman 1987. Who influences strategic decisions? *Long Range Planning* **20**, 2, 54–69.

Jackson, P. & K. Sisson 1975. Management and collective bargaining – a framework for an international comparison of employer organizations. Industrial Relations Research Unit, University of Warwick, mimeo.

Knights, D., H. Wilmot & D. Collinson 1985. *Job Redesign: Critical Perspectives on the Labour Process*. London: Gower.

Kochan, T., H. Katz & R. McKersie 1986. *The Transformation of American Industrial Relations.* New York: Basic Books.

Littler, C. 1982. *The Development of the Labour Process in Capitalist Societies; A Comparative Study of the Transformation of Work Organization in Britain, Japan and the USA.* London: Heinemann.

Littler, C. 1987. Labour process literature: a review 1974–1986. In *Contemporary Industrial Relations in Australia and New Zealand: Literature Surveys,* K. Hince & A. Williams (eds), 57–100. New Zealand, AIRAANZ and Industrial Relations Centre, Victoria University.

Littler, C. & G. Salaman 1982. Bravermania and beyond: recent theories of the labour process. *Sociology* **16**, 251–69.

McCaffree, K. 1962. A theory of the origin and development of employer associations. *Proceedings of the 15th Annual Meeting of the Industrial Relations Research Association,* 56–68. Pittsburgh, Pa: Industrial Relations Research Association.

McGregor, D. 1960. *The Human Side of the Enterprise.* New York: McGraw-Hill.

Munson, F. 1962. National association bargaining in the lithographic industry. *Proceedings of the 15th Annual Meeting of the Industrial Relations Research Association,* 83–91. Pittsburgh, Pa: Industrial Relations Research Association.

Phelps Brown, E. H. 1959. *The Growth of British Industrial Relations.* London: Macmillan.

Plowman, D. 1983. Employer associations: a research strategy. In *Industrial Relations Teaching and Research in Australia and New Zealand,* J. Benson (ed.), 261–304. Melbourne: AIRAANZ.

Plowman, D. 1987. Employer associations: a literature review. In *Contemporary Industrial Relations in Australia and New Zealand: Literature Surveys,* K. Hince & A. Williams (eds), 199–228. New Zealand, AIRAANZ and Industrial Relations Centre, Victoria University.

Plowman, D. 1988. *Holding the Line: Compulsory Arbitration and National Employer Co-ordination in Australia.* Sydney: Cambridge University Press.

Purcell, J. 1983. Management control through collective bargaining: a future strategy. In *Industrial Relations and Management Strategy,* K. Thurley & S. Wood (eds), 1–16. Cambridge: Cambridge University Press.

Purcell, J. 1987. Mapping management styles in employee relations. *Journal of Management Studies* **24**, 5, September, 533–48.

Purcell, J. & B. Ahlstrand 1988. Business strategy and employee relations structures in the multi-divisional company. Oxford: Templeton College, mimeo.

Purcell, J. & K. Sisson 1983. Strategies and practice in the management of industrial relations. In *Industrial Relations in Britain,* G. S. Bain (ed.), 95–120. Oxford: Blackwell.

Report of Royal Commission on Trade Unions and Employers' Associations, 1967. London: HMSO.

Rose, M. & B. Jones 1985. Managerial strategy and trade union responses to work organization schemes at the establishment level. In *Job Redesign:*

Critical Perspectives on the Labour Process, D. H. Knights, H. Wilmot & D. Collinson (eds). London: Gower.

Sisson, K. 1986. A comparative analysis of the structure of collective bargaining. In *Alternatives to Arbitration*, R. Blandy & J. Niland (eds), 183–99. Sydney: Allen and Unwin.

Slate, D. M. 1957. Trade union behaviour and the local employers' association. *Industrial and Labor Relations Review* **11**, 1.

Storey, J. 1983. *Managerial Prerogative and the Question of Control*. London: Routledge & Kegan Paul.

Streeck, W. 1982. Between pluralism and corporatism, German business associations and the state. Paper presented at the IPSA World Congress, Rio de Janeiro, August, mimeo.

Tomlinson J. 1982. *The Unequal Struggle*. London: Macmillan.

Webb, Sidney & Beatrice Webb 1897. *Industrial Democracy*. New York: Longmans, Green.

Wood, S. (ed.) 1982. *The Degradation of Work?* London: Hutchinson.

Wood, S. & R. Elliot 1977. A critical evaluation of Fox's radicalization in industrial relations. *Sociology* **11**.

Woodward, J. 1970. *Industrial Organization: Behaviour and Control*. Oxford: Oxford University Press.

6 The role of the state as corporate actor in industrial relations systems

BERNDT K. KELLER

Introduction

The vast majority of our analytical concepts and tools which try to theorize in the interdisciplinary field of industrial relations agree on one general hypothesis although they are derived from quite different theoretical perspectives (systems theory, pluralism, Marxism, among others): we should explicitly set out from (or at least implicitly deal with) three key corporate actors and their formal and informal inter-relationships:

- workers and trade unions as the representatives of their interests;
- managers, employers and their associations; and
- the state (including, among others, various government agencies, federal and state governments, and labour courts).

Most industrial relations theory and empirical research focuses on the bipartite relationship between workers and management (including their associations). The third and equally important corporate actor, the state, is comparatively neglected. (Two of the rare attempts to place the state in theoretical perspective are Dabscheck 1983 and Giles 1988.)

At first glance, this neglect might not seem to create serious problems because of the primary interest of IR scholars in labour-management relations. However, this point of view must be seen as limited to treatment of industrial relations in those countries (like the United Kingdom) where the state has traditionally played a minor and non-decisive role in industrial relations, being basically limited to providing an institutional framework for bilateral relations between management and labour. This obvious bias does, however, cause major shortcomings if we try to transfer these analytical concepts to research on other Western industrialized nations. Many have a history of significant and crucial involvement of the state, and systems of collective bargaining are highly centralized. Examples are Austria, some Scandinavian countries, and West Germany.

The deficiency of theory with regard to the state has produced an over-concentration in contemporary industrial relations discourse on elements in union policy and the problems facing unions such as losses of membership, declining degrees of organization, difficulties with regard to the introduction of new technologies at plant level, more competition on the rapidly changing world markets, and the need to fight mass unemployment. Additional analyses provide general information and guided speculation on the future activities and policies of management and employers (see e.g. Edwards *et al.* 1986, Lipset 1986, Müller-Jentsch 1988).

In order to address the conceptual gap in the literature, I will offer some initial ideas on the role of the state. I shall concentrate on current and future rather than historical developments and problems (on the historical development of collective bargaining regulations in selected countries see Bean 1985, and on the history of the relationship between the state and unions see Tomlins 1985; in a more comparative perspective, Rimlinger 1977).

My focus will be on governments and their strategic choices (Kochan *et al.* 1984), including their decisive interaction with the other corporate actors in formulating and implementing public policies. Other components of the state – in particular, parliaments and the routinized processes of decision-making within the legal system (with its typical interpretation, administration and implementation of the existing labour law), and those other parts of the network of state institutions which fulfil special functions – are less relevant and will not explicitly be dealt with. In this way, the complications of different problems of internal decision-making and conflict within the corporate actor can be avoided. The general focus of my analysis will be on Western market economies, deliberately excluding communist and developing countries.

Historical roles and general functions of the state

The general industrial relations literature gives us scattered information on some of the historical roles and major general functions of the state as described below.

* In all countries more or less comprehensive systems of individual and collective *labour law* have been gradually developed in the process of industrialization. The general aim was to regulate the conflictual relationships between management and labour at various levels (the enterprise, the region, and the whole economy), in order to protect labour and to achieve a balance by adjustment of the legal environment. There are, however, for historical and other reasons, considerable national diversities in the form and structure of legal systems and intervention in the *laissez-faire* economy. The Australian and German legal systems, for example, are well known for their high degree of legalistic intervention ('juridification'). The United Kingdom was, for an extended period until the 1970s, a clear contrast, being characterized by almost complete legal abstention and voluntarism.
* Quite often these general legal frameworks also include some substantive provisions for universal *minimum standards of conditions of employment* (such as minimum wages, limitation or standardization of daily or weekly working hours, occupational safety and health provisions, anti-discrimination regulations, vacations, and protection against dismissal). The general alternative, or sometimes even supplementary mechanism for setting these general terms of employment by non-political means, is collective bargaining (in the United Kingdom and United States, for example). This way is, of course, only effective if trade unions have sufficient strength and power.
* In all developed Western nations the state has always tried to avoid or at least limit collective *industrial conflicts* after the general right to strike was legally guaranteed. Action has been taken to curb both official and unofficial strikes, and sometimes also lock-outs, in order to protect the general 'public' from (real or imagined) harmful (or even 'disastrous') consequences. In some countries (the United Kingdom and the United States among others) governments themselves are responsible for institutions and mechanisms of third-party conflict resolution in the

private and public sector, as well. Procedural rules for mediation, conciliation and even voluntary or compulsory arbitration
processes are externally provided for by the state. In other
countries dispute settlement procedures internally organized by
the parties themselves are strongly encouraged and supported
by the state.

- In many North American and European countries (but not
  including France and Italy) there are strict and legally enforced
  obligations to keep the peace during a period governed by a
  collective contract. Here clear distinctions are made: individual
  and collective *conflicts of rights* (about the interpretation of an
  existing collective agreement) are in most cases to be solved by
  peaceful, legal means including labour court decisions, and not
  by private grievance procedures. On the other hand, all *conflicts
  of interest* (about the terms of a new contract) involve different
  methods of conflict resolution including industrial action. Under
  this kind of legal framework some forms of strike can be and
  often are declared illegal.
- Various public agencies are actively involved in *public sector
  labour relations*, because the state and other public authorities
  are direct employers of a large percentage of the labour force.
  This number increased steadily for quite some decades. Thus
  public authorities can exert a significant amount of influence
  not only on this particular sector, but also on the development
  of the overall industrial relations system. A whole set of difficult
  problems resulting from this particular role is well known and
  documented in the international industrial relations literature of
  the last 20 years or so. These include growing unionization, the
  disputed right to strike – typically excluding particular groups
  with crucial functions, various procedures of dispute settlements,
  different methods of income regulation (see e.g. *Proceedings...
  of the International Industrial Relations Association* 1986, Treu
  1987). Because of this vast amount of specialized literature
  on different aspects of public sector industrial relations I will
  concentrate on the private sector and the problem in general.

The general observations made above indicate significant cross-
national differences in quantitative and qualitative terms of past and
current governmental interference. In the long run a clear trend in
all advanced capitalist countries may be observed towards more
frequent and more systematic active governmental intervention in

the industrial relations system. This long-term development includes the active legislative encouragement of collective bargaining in an early period and, at a more recent stage, more or less active labour market policies and macro-economic strategies designed to stabilize growth or to fight unemployment.

It seems, though, as if this trend of increasing regulatory and distributive policies and of management of the economy by the interventionist state may be coming to an end. Strategies of deregulation, initiated mainly by conservative governments, indicate a reversal of this trend (see the section on *Threats and challenges*, 83–6). Enormous diversities between different national policies can be observed.

In conventional industrial relations theory we usually differentiate between procedural and substantive norms. The long-term trend can be described as a movement towards more encompassing substantive rules, quite often imposed by the state in terms of legal interference. But the new industrial relations of the 1990s likely will be characterized by an increasing importance of, if not domination by, procedural rules and regulations which permit more 'flexibility' to managerial decision-makers.

Macro-corporatism: a temporary mode of regulation

While discussions of the state are often impressionistic and descriptive, more cohesive and theoretically oriented analysis is to be found in the still ongoing discussion on neo-corporatism. This thrust has been led mainly by political scientists and political sociologists only occasionally joined by specialists in industrial relations themselves.

Generally speaking, models of corporatism, the 'growth industry' of the 1970s, are the well-known attempt:

- to bring the autonomous and independent state with its, nowadays, more active, direct intervention in the economic processes and their material results back to the centre of the stage; and
- to analyse in more theoretical terms some recent integrative and co-operative trends within the system of interest representation, mainly of interest intermediation within the institutionalized structure of industrial relations.

After the Second World War, but mainly in the 1960s and early 1970s, representative systems between governments and the leaders of the main interest groups of capital and labour came into existence in several liberal democracies (Crouch 1978, Maier 1984). This form of organizational and political interest intermediation and conflict resolution gradually replaced classic, more pluralistic and liberal forms of industrial relations by centralized, institutionalized and more co-ordinated types of interest politics. 'Ostensibly corporatism provides an ideal solution to the central problem of modern capitalism: the maintenance of order where market relations are no longer supreme, where the division between polity and economy can no longer be sustained, and where both the working class and capital are organized' (Crouch 1978: 215).

Institutional provisions for the relative, but temporary success of this broad neo-corporatist concertation in at least some countries seem to be (Schmitter & Lehmbruch 1979, Lehmbruch & Schmitter 1982):

- unitarian and highly centralized systems of interest representation with corresponding, non-fragmented structures of corporate decision-making within and between organizations;
- the factual right of associations to act as exclusive representatives, to exert sufficient social control over the behaviour of their rank and file in order to carry out mutual obligations, and to participate in public policy-making, i.e. economic planning in general and incomes policy in particular;
- a clear domination of industrial unionism as the dominating organizational principle over more fragmented union structures:
- and governments léd by Labour or Social Democrats with their typical institutional links, strong personal ties, overlapping memberships, and ideological affiliations. These include sufficient political consensus with 'their' loyal trade unions. Austria can be taken as a prototypical example, especially contrasted with the highly decentralized US system.

Governments in various capitalist countries have quite often tried to initiate, maintain and make use of these widespread tripartite institutions (Juris *et al.* 1985). These include those in Austria, the Netherlands and some Scandinavian countries. Australia before 1985 (cf. on recent trends Frenkel 1988), the United Kingdom under Thatcher and the United States under Reagan were definitely not included. Canada seemed to be moving away from the North American pattern and towards tripartist arrangements of the European type of concerted socioeconomic decision-making during the 1970s but that trend is no longer evident in the 1980s (see Adams 1985 and the Thompson chapter in this volume). Somewhere in between these extremes are Italy and France.

This co-operation at the national level between government and the heads of the main organizations of capital and labour was intended to cope with the whole range of problems of managing the Keynesian welfare state. It was intended to achieve relative stability of prices, distribution of income including incomes policy and wage restraint by trade unions, and steady economic growth and, later on, to solve the problem of maintaining full employment. In an international comparison the degrees of severity of intervention into 'free' collective bargaining were quite varied (indicative, imperative, and co-operative forms); a whole range of institutional forms were to be observed (Beyme 1977: 243–62).

In the 1970s governments urgently needed voluntary assistance and 'responsible' co-operation of autonomous trade unions and their leaders for the successful management of strategies for macro-economic stabilization. These strategies included, first of all, incomes policies and wage restraint by the unions and the workers. This co-operation was required in an extended period of rapid economic growth and rising national prosperity. On the other hand, governments had to grant their 'partners' something in political exchange, as compensation for their incorporation and societal integration. Results and consequences of these implicit or even explicit social contracts within bargained corporatism included:

- more and improved rights to co-determination and participation;
- fulfilment of certain social policy demands, in particular expansion of the welfare state; and
- more political influence in the process of political give and take.

The overall result was that trade unions became more powerful. They gained official and integrative recognition within the political system, had effective access to 'their' governments and exerted considerable influence on national policies as 'social partners' within this restructured distribution of power (Pizzorno 1978).

Threats and challenges

This mode of argument rests more on the approaches of exchange theory and methodological individualism than on theoretical stances such as Marxist interpretations of the function of the state in advanced capitalist societies based on class-theoretical considerations (see OECD 1982, Lehmbruch 1984 and Lange 1984 for the former, Strinati 1979 and Panitch 1980 for the latter alternative). I assume, of course, that all corporate participants act with subjective rationality and calculate strategically the subjective costs and benefits of their ongoing participation in such more or less voluntary experiments. They act according to their own interest in that they follow the strategy that maximizes the subjective expected utilities of their organizations. All partners have in principle the option to 'exit' at any point in time if they come to the conclusion that their positive compensations have deteriorated. Neo-corporatist arrangements can succeed only when every necessary actor continues to participate. Tripartite structures are eventually abandoned where they do not yield a net profit any more for their corporate participants. Therefore, all such corporate networks, both at national and regional level, are highly unstable (Streit 1988).

One of the basic problems has always been the empirically observed fact that trade union leaders run into enormous internal difficulties when they agree, in accord with consensual wage policies, to administer some sort of wage restraint. At exactly the same time governments are often unable to control by political means all other variables of macro-economic importance, such as consumer prices, profits, and investments.

Because of these difficulties unions have in the past often threatened to leave and in some cases actually have left these tripartite institutions. 'Instances can be readily cited ... in which corporatist arrangements have collapsed either as a result of the withdrawal of union leaders or of their inability to "deliver" their rank and file' (Goldthorpe 1984: 336; also OECD 1982: 46). Today, in a period of rapid economic transformation and political changes, both conservative governments and employers have begun to recalculate their positions with the result that the main threats to neo-corporatist pacts currently are management and, under certain political circumstances, government.

Quite a few of the regulative and integrative arrangements of the 'Golden Age' of societal corporatism seem to have gradually disappeared over the period of declining economic performance starting in the mid-1970s and during the rise of a more flexible form of 'post-Fordist' capitalism, and of 'flexible specialization' (Piore & Sabel 1984) in the 1980s.

Unfortunately we do not know very much about alternative management strategies. There is no 'sociology of management' to be applied in different national contexts. But the initiative of strategic action that had been more on the unions' side for quite some decades after the Second World War has, in the recent past, again been taken over by management and employers. They are pushing vigorously for industrial 'adjustment', i.e. more flexible conditions of production generally, and more flexibility with regard to the 'institutional rigidities' of the labour market in particular. These include demands for fewer legal constraints, less rigidity of wages, more flexibilization of working-time arrangements, and other working conditions.

Management opts for wide-ranging provisions of 'flexibilization' of almost all terms of employment in order to support the ongoing processes of economic recovery and reconstruction. But: 'This authoritarian non-union strategy is generally justified on the basis that it is more efficient economically than is democratic participation by right. There is, however, little objective evidence to support that proposition' (Adams 1985: 146).

These economic factors blend, of course, with significant *changes in the political sphere*. The general tendency towards a new imbalance of power and fundamental change in overall political orientation has been clearly strengthened by the departure of many labour and social democratic parties from power and their replacement by neo-conservative governments.

Thus, the essential condition of macro-corporatism, the offer by the state to management *and* labour to participate in the process of socioeconomic decision-making, has been eroded in at least some countries (among others, the United Kingdom and to a lesser degree West Germany). On the other hand, corporatist institutions continued to function in those countries (Austria, Sweden) where personal links, political ties and ideological affiliations between trade unions and the government remained stable. If tripartism had been institutionalized before conservative governments came into power the chances of survival were fair. It is extremely difficult though to generalize from nation-specific peculiarities.

At the same time as employers started their strategies of flexibilization, conservative governments initiated political provisions towards gradual 'deregulation' of parts of the existing industrial relations system. These measures aimed, first of all, at parts of the traditional labour law which regulated employment conditions, such as the right to lay off, and to transfer employees.

Thus, economic (labour market developments and rapid technological change) and political factors (change of political majorities) worked in the same direction, eroding unions' bargaining power and political strength. These trends do not necessarily belong together but, in fact, they have occurred at almost the same time. Governmental deregulation strategies definitely reinforce management's initiatives for more 'flexibility'.

European employers' organizations have been lobbying quite successfully for governmental and legislative protection of their plans for change. Generally this is easier to achieve with conservative governments and legislatures (see the national studies in Windmuller & Gladstone 1986). Even without these political changes the economic trend would still have made the situation difficult but easier to handle for the trade unions.

At the regional and national levels of many countries trade unions do not have very much to offer any more as a political exchange. Mass unemployment following the second oil price shock has significantly weakened unions' organizational and bargaining power in almost all important sectors of the national economies. Trade unions cannot expect very much support from conservative governments, which mistrust any sort of corporatist solutions since these are based on political mediation of interest rather than their preferred mode of regulation – the market. These governments believe wholeheartedly in privatization and in the 'invisible hand'. The United States and the United Kingdom are good examples again. The aim is to improve productivity and their own position on the world markets, and to become more competitive. In some cases, formal bargaining structures and even informal contacts and other mediating exchanges between governments and trade unions have been reduced to an absolute minimum. An exchange of views, consensus and union participation are no longer considered necessary or desirable.

Corporatist solutions are definitely not a question of either this or that, but of more or less. However, the overall direction is quite obvious. Market types of conflict resolution are becoming more and more substitutes for corporatist arrangements within a neo-conservative, more traditional style of general politics and renewed liberal *laissez-faire* industrial relations politics.

Conservative governments are, however, far from being unitary and there is an enormous, probably even growing and accelerating degree of variation between national strategies towards deregulation and de-institutionalization (Lash & Bagguley 1988). Some governments clearly follow a strategy of weakening the status and integrity of organized labour, others are more cautious and less aggressive. This variation reflects fundamental differences within and between the corporate actors, political conditions and perceptions about the unions' strength and the degree to which they are embedded in the social structure as well. We have only to think of 'labour exclusion' strategies in the United Kingdom and of 'union avoidance' in the United States as one end of a continuum, at the other end of which lie Austria and West Germany, with their very modest changes in the collective and individual parts of their labour law.

In general, political attacks on the legitimate institutions of trade unions and on formalized rights and rules seem to be more successful and far-reaching where trade unions as institutions are not highly centralized (in the organizational pattern of industrial unionism) and where labour rights are hardly institutionalized legally in a system of participation and co-determination. These differences may clearly be seen in comparing, for example, the United Kingdom and the United States, with their clear trends of destabilization and erosion, with West Germany, Sweden and Austria, countries characterized by continuity and relative stability. Strong and highly centralized trade unions, with fixed legal rights of participation and co-determination and collective bargaining at both enterprise and regional or national level, seem to be much better equipped to meet fundamental attacks than decentralized and weaker organizations with fewer formalized rights such as are found in the United States.

Micro-corporatism – no need for the state?

In some cases, the tripartite macro-corporatist pacts at the national and regional levels of the economy have been replaced by bipartite, so-called micro-corporatist arrangements or productivity alliances (Windolf 1989). These either renewed or new modes of micro-regulation consist of very 'high trust/low conflict relations' which mutually further the interests and advantages of both management *and* labour. There are gains on both sides in employment security and productivity, as well as increased flexibility of the internal, firm-specific labour market. These pacts include facets of integrative bargaining (in the sense Walton & McKersie 1965 coined this expression). These exchange agreements appear to be quite stable and difficult to break up. These relatively autonomous alliances seem, at first glance at least, to be viable without continuous state participation or active interference although the general framework for their existence often has been set up or at least encouraged by state agencies.

Typically, the negative consequences of collective action are externalized. The result is high entrance barriers to the internal, firm-specific labour market and a widening gap between the employed and the unemployed parts of the labour force. This creates problems at the macro-level, such as persistent or rising unemployment, increasing processes of segmentation, or, if not and, dualization within and between different labour markets. These are unintended consequences of rational and collective action at the micro-level of the enterprise.

These recent syndicalistic developments can be interpreted as a definite and clear *tendency towards the decentralization of industrial relations*. This is especially (but definitely not only, see Lash & Bagguley 1988, Windolf 1989) true in those countries characterized by highly centralized industrial relations systems in the past. Again the collective bargaining systems in Austria and West Germany are good examples. The ongoing processes of introduction and implementation of new technologies which demand specific and flexible adaptation at the enterprise and work-place level have reinforced the trend to decentralization. So too has the negotiation of specific formulas for the reduction in weekly working time in some countries.

Some speculations about the future of state intervention

Even tentative prognoses are extremely difficult in the field of industrial relations, especially in a period of fundamental transformation and rapid change.

Differences within and between the industrial relations systems of various nations likely will continue to increase. In the foreseeable future, the state will possibly play a less dominant role than it did in the Keynesian welfare period when governments tried (more or less successfully) to manage the vital, macro-level problems of economic growth, employment, price stability, etc. The Tayloristic–Fordist 'period of standardized mass production' seems to be ending in the 'second industrial divide', the phase of 'flexible specialization' (Piore & Sabel 1984). This new, changed mode of production seems, at first glance at least, not to require as much systematic legal or political intervention by the state.

New modes of regulation at the plant and enterprise levels are going to influence strongly the industrial relations of the 1990s. The introduction and implementation of new technologies could generate problems of decisive importance. Technological developments, the introduction of micro-electronics as a new basic technology, clearly favour changes in the direction of flexibilization and differentiation. Conservative political trends, if they continue, will leave the trade unions without a strong and reliable partner for political bargaining. Therefore, unions will, all in all, find themselves in a more defensive position than in the past; they will react rather than take the lead. Another serious problem European unions will face is whether to represent the employed parts of the labour force at the level of the firm or continue to be an encompassing institution (including the unemployed) representing broad class instead of narrow sectional interests. This is a clear and obvious difference in comparison with the decades following the Second World War.

There seem to be at least two possible solutions for the future relationship between the state and the other social partners.

• Under conservative leadership a likely scenario would be: in those countries where the state was comparatively dominant in the recent past its influence could be significantly lessened in the foreseeable future. In countries where the state did not play a dominant role in industrial relations in the past its role will not change significantly but change will again be towards a lesser role. Management will in all cases be supported by legal and other means. The attack on unions – imposing 'rigid' rules – could be continued. The United Kingdom is a good example for this alternative.

- Social democratic governments, with non-conservative political priorities would, if they could win the majority of votes, rather try to create new, balanced forms of tripartite strategies and institutions, including industrial policy. These strategies would be unlikely to re-establish the status quo ante, but instead would be likely to support the introduction and implementation of 'new production and employment concepts' (Kern & Schumann 1984, 1987) while avoiding serious social conflicts and industrial unrest. The relative importance of unions would rise, compared to management. The introduction and implementation of advanced technologies would be the central new field of political control. Legal intervention would favour improved and enlarged rights of institutionalized participation and, maybe, even co-determination. Training and retraining of the employed and unemployed segments of the workforce would be another steadily growing arena for public policy (Keller 1989). In general, a renewed institutional, less restricted, newly balanced framework would be likely to be constructed under changed political circumstances.

The fundamental differences for the years to come will not be whether the processes of decentralization of union–management decision-making are going to continue or not. This decision has already been made. In the highly centralized bargaining systems of some Western European nations the trends towards decentralization will be more obvious and far-reaching than in more decentralized ones such as the United States and the United Kingdom. However, this is only a gradual difference, not a difference in kind. All in all, decentralization makes any kind of state control more difficult, but definitely not superfluous. Sweden is the typical example of a social democratic government that has thrown its weight against the tide of decentralization.

Recent studies converge on the conclusion that the direction of these innovative processes of non-Tayloristic rationalization can be influenced and even changed by political means (Kern & Schumann 1984, Piore & Sabel 1984). Thus, the fundamental political problem will be whether these ongoing processes of decentralization will take place under some sort of political – and therefore social – control by the state. Governments will have to decide – probably under the growing pressure of even more urgent problems – whether to formulate a legal frame of reference or leave these processes to the forces of the 'invisible hand' of the 'free' market.

This would leave no effective legal protection of the weaker groups, those with little or no bargaining power, who are exposed to less pluralistic, maybe even dualistic, structures of labour markets and to fragmented industrial relations. There is evidence that this development will result in strong tendencies towards increasing societal segmentation, deeper status differences, and a growing disparity of living conditions (Kern & Schumann 1984, Baethge & Oberbeck 1986).

Outlook

Last but not least, what do all these structural developments in the real world mean for future research and for industrial relations theory? First of all, we should take more seriously the fact that industrial relations systems are composed of three corporate actors. This fact includes the necessity to analyse state activities on the vertical axis (aiming at the other actors) *and* on the horizontal axis (within different state agencies) as well. We know, for example, too little about the interactive relationship between the government and the judicial system in different countries.

The described processes of deregulation and flexibilization will make the theoretical and empirical analysis more complex than it has been in the past. Generalizations between sectors of a national industrial relations system or between national industrial relations systems will be more difficult in the future.

One factor of significant importance in the foreseeable future will have to do with the *internationalization of the Western European economies* including common internal markets not only for all goods and services but also for labour in 1992. All corporate actors are poorly prepared for the social problems created by the political integration of different national economies.

This political strategy of unification will increase the ongoing liberalization and 'deregulation' of all national labour markets. This will require an internationalization of trade unions and their nationally oriented and divided politics: e.g. collective bargaining including mediation procedures, rights of co-determination, minimum standards of employment. National economic and industrial relations policies, including employment policy, will matter less in the 1990s than they ever did in the past: a new arena of politics (so-called multi- or transnational European politics) will become of increasing importance for all corporate actors within the industrial relations system – including the national states. A certain European standardization and harmonization of all national rules and regulations seems to be necessary but extremely difficult to achieve. This will be a task of decisive importance for the European Parliament – and should not be simply left to the social partners.

References

Adams, R. J. 1985. Industrial relations and the economic crisis: Canada moves towards Europe. In *Industrial Relations in a Decade of Economic Change*, H. Juris *et al.* (eds), 115–49. Madison, Wisc.: Industrial Relations Research Association.

Baethge, M. & H. Oberbeck 1986. *Zukunft der Angestellten. Neue Technologien und Berufliche Perspektiven' in Büro und Verwaltung*. Frankfurt & New York.

Bean, R. 1985. *Comparative Industrial Relations – An Introduction to Cross-National Perspectives*. London: Croom Helm.

Beyme, K. V. 1977. *Gewerkschaften und Arbeitsbeziehungen in Kapitalistischen Länder*. Munich.

Crouch, C. 1978. The changing role of the state in industrial relations in western Europe. In *The Resurgence of Class Conflict in Western Europe since 1968*, C. Crouch & A. Pizzorno (eds). Vol. 2, *Comparative Analysis*. 197–220. New York: Holmes & Meier.

Dabscheck, B. 1983. Of mountains and routes over them: a survey of theories of industrial relations. *Journal of Industrial Relations* **25**, 485–506.

Edwards, R., P. Garonna, & F. Tödtling (eds) 1986. *Unions in Crisis and Beyond: Perspectives From Six Countries*. London: Auburn House.

Frenkel, S. J. 1988. Australian employers in the shadow of the labour accords. *Industrial Relations* **27**, 166–79.

Giles, A. 1988. Industrial relations theory, the state and politics. In *Theories and Concepts of Industrial Relations*, J. Barbash (ed.), 123–54. Columbia, SC: University of South Carolina Press.

Goldthorpe, J. H. 1984. The end of convergence: corporatist and dualist tendencies in modern western societies. In *Order and Conflict in Contemporary Capitalism*, J. H. Goldthorpe (ed.), 315–43. Oxford: Clarendon.

Juris, H., M. Thompson, & W. Daniels (eds), 1985. *Industrial Relations in a Decade of Economic Change*. Madison, Wisc.: Industrial Relations Research Association.

Keller, B. 1989. Krise der institutionellen Interessenvermittlung und Zukunft (der Arbeitsbeziehungen: Flexibilisierung. Deregulierung. Mikrokorporatismus. In *Macht und Ohnmacht Politischer Institutionen*, H. H. Hartwich (ed.), 135–57. Tagungsband des DVPW-Kongresses 1988, Opladen.

Kern, H. & M. Schumann 1984. *Das Ende der Arbeitsteilung? Rationalisierung in der Industriellen Massenproduktion.* Munich.

Kern, H. & M. Schumann 1987. Limits of the division of labour. New production and employment concepts in West German industry. *Economic and Industrial Democracy* **8**, 151–70.

Kochan, T., R. B. McKersie, & P. Cappelli 1984. Strategic choice and industrial relations theory. *Industrial Relations* **23**, 16–39.

Lange, P. 1984. Unions, workers and wage regulation: the rational bases of consent. In *Order and Conflict in Contemporary Capitalism*, J. H. Goldthorpe (ed.), 98–123. Oxford: Clarendon.

Lash, S. & P. Bagguley 1988. Arbeitsbeziehungen im disorganisierten Kapitalismus: ein Vergleich von fünf Nationen. *Soziale Welt* **39**, 239–59.

Lehmbruch, G. Concertation and the structure of corporatist networks. In *Order and Conflict in Contemporary Capitalism*, J. H. Goldthorpe (ed.), 60–80. Oxford: Clarendon.

Lehmbruch, G. & P. C. Schmitter (eds) 1982. *Patterns of Corporatist Policy-making.* Beverly Hills, Calif.: Sage.

Lipset, S. M. (ed.) 1986. *Unions in Transition: Entering the Second Century.* San Francisco: ICS Press.

Maier, C. S. 1984. Preconditions for corporatism. In *Order and Conflict in Contemporary Capitalism*, J. H. Goldthorpe (ed.), 39–59. Oxford: Clarendon.

Müller-Jentsch, W. (ed.) 1988. *Zukunft der Gewerkschaften. Ein Internationaler Vergleich.* Frankfurt.

OECD 1982. *The Search for Consensus. The Role of Institutional Dialogue between Government, Labour and Employers.* Paris.

Panitch, L. 1980. Recent theorizations of corporatism: reflections on a growth industry. *British Journal of Sociology* **31**, 159–87.

Piore, M. J. & C. F. Sabel 1984. *The Second Industrial Divide: Possibilities for Prosperity.* New York: Basic Books.

Pizzorno, A. 1978. Political exchange and collective identity in industrial conflict. In *The Resurgence of Class Conflict in Western Europe since 1986*, C. Crouch & A. Pizzorno (eds). Vol. 2, *Comparative Analysis*, 277–98. London: Holmes & Meier.

Poole, M. 1986. *Industrial Relations: Origins and Patterns of National Diversity.* London: Routledge & Kegan Paul.

Proceedings of the Seventh World Congress of the International Industrial Relations Association. 1986. Vol. IV: *Co-operation and Conflict in Public Service Labour Relations.* Geneva: International Industrial Relations Association.

Rimlinger, G. 1977. Labour and the government: a comparative historical perspective. *Journal of Economic History* **37**, 210–25.

Schmitter, P.C. & G. Lehmbruch (eds) 1979. *Trends Towards Corporatist Intermediation.* London: Sage.

Streit, M. E. 1988. The mirage of neo-corporatism. *Kyklos* **41**, 603–24.

Strinati, D. 1979. Capitalism, the state and industrial relations. In *State and Economy in Contemporary Capitalism*, C. Crouch (ed.), 191–236. London: St Martin's Press.

Strinati, D. 1982. *Capitalism, the State and Industrial Relations*. London & Canberra: Croom Helm.

Tomlins, C. 1985. *The State and the Unions. Labour Relations, Law, and the Organized Labour Movement in America, 1880–1960*. New York: Cambridge University Press.

Treu, T. (ed.) 1987. *Public Service Labour Relations: Recent Trends and Future Prospects. A Comparative Survey of Seven Industrialized Market Economy Countries*. Geneva: International Labour Office.

Walton, R. E. & R. B. McKersie 1965. *A Behavioural Theory of Labour Negotiations: An Analysis of a Social Interaction System*. New York: McGraw-Hill.

Windmuller, J. P. & A. Gladstone (eds) 1986. *Employers' Associations and Industrial Relations. A Comparative Study*. 2nd edn. Oxford: Clarendon.

Windolf, P. 1989. Productivity coalitions and the future of corporatism. A comparative view on western European industrial relations. *Industrial Relations* **28**, 1–20.

7 Union–management relations: recent research and theory

MARK THOMPSON

During the past decade, both the environment and the conduct of industrial relations have changed substantially. For the previous 40 years, there was an implicit assumption in developed countries that the well-being and rights of workers would improve on a secular basis, usually led by those sectors where formal collective bargaining structures existed. In most Western industrialized nations, these assumptions were challenged in the 1980s, with profound results for the practice of industrial relations, its study and the theory guiding research.

A significant trend in the 1980s in many countries has been the retreat of collective bargaining, either in terms of its extent or of the impact of its results. If one takes union membership as a general proxy for the extent of collective bargaining, the institution shrank by over 10 per cent in the United States and the United Kingdom between 1981 and 1986, and declined in relative terms in Australia, France, Japan and the Netherlands (Kumar *et al.* 1988). Apart from the extent of the institution, the leading role of the unionized sector in setting terms of employment diminished in these and other nations. In addition, there were major changes in collective bargaining in those sectors where it remained a vigorous institution.

It would be impossible in a chapter of this length to discuss all of the recent literature on collective bargaining in all countries, so this review will concentrate on research published in the 1980s in developed nations, focusing on the trends in industrial relations mentioned above.

Industrial relations has always been a relatively atheoretical field, although the body of theory is much more extensive than many scholars seem able to admit. With one or two exceptions, no general theories of industrial relations phenomena have been proposed in recent years. However, the explicit formulation of theoretical propositions is a growing concern in industrial relations research, and attention to the task of building industrial relations theory appears to be increasing (see Kochan *et al.* 1984, Capelli 1985, Adams 1988, Reshef & Murray 1988, Poole 1988, Turnbull 1988, Kirkbride 1985, Gospel 1983, Larouche & Déom 1984, Shirom 1985, Dabschek 1980, Audet & Larouche 1988, Fulcher 1988). In addition, a considerable body of theory underlies much of the work reviewed here.

For purposes of this chapter, 'industrial relations theory' will include efforts to explain relationships between independent and dependent variables in ways that lend themselves to generalization and generate further hypotheses about the significant features of the field, i.e. relations among organized workers and their employers and government (see Heneman 1969). The focus in this chapter is collective bargaining and related institutions.

The decline of corporatism

The diminished importance of collective bargaining was felt at various levels where negotiations take place. While the parties in North America and Japan are accustomed to bargaining at the industry level or lower, in Europe, negotiations and consultation by the industrial relations parties with government developed in the years after the Second World War. The scope of these arrangements varied, but often included macro-economic policy as well as terms and conditions of employment. During the 1970s, these institutions were analysed through the corporatist paradigm (see Beaumont 1988).

The corporatist model encouraged researchers to go beyond descriptions of arrangements for consultation and policy formulation to generate hypotheses and a body of theory. Questions were raised concerning the relationship between corporatism and other forms of worker participation, for instance. The influence of links between unions and political parties on bargaining was explored, among other topics.

During the 1980s, corporatist arrangements weakened or disappeared in a number of countries, such as the United Kingdom, the

Netherlands, and Sweden (Lash & Urry 1987), while a new system of national consultation linking industrial relations and economic policy was implemented in Australia (Thompson & Juris 1985). Even in the United States, an informal social contract which existed between the AFL–CIO and the Federal government was virtually eliminated under the Reagan administration (Edwards & Podgursky, 1986). In the 1970s a liberal Canadian government attempted to establish corporatist systems of intermediation (Adams 1985); in the following decade a more conservative Federal government showed little sustained interest in such consultation.

Analyses of the causes of the break-up of corporatist systems focused on both economic and political variables. Increased unemployment undermined employer interest in negotiating wage policies with labour centrals, since the need for trade union wage restraint had been diminished, if not eliminated. When occasional labour market shortages occurred, employers preferred to address these problems on a decentralized basis. Several countries elected governments with a philosophical preference for market regulation, further weakening national negotiations (Lash 1985, Goldthorpe 1984).

While theoretical bases for the emergence and decline of corporatism have been well explained, new types of relationships between the state and industrial relations parties (especially the labour movement) offer a challenging field of research for industrial relations scholars (Gourevitch *et al.* 1984). If governments reduce the extent of their intervention in labour matters, the utility of the political science paradigms is likely to diminish accordingly. Yet increasing reliance on the market does not offer obvious opportunities for the application of economic theory to macro-level industrial relations. Efforts to construct new theories to explain emerging patterns of interest-group relations have had limited impact on industrial relations (see Goldthorpe 1984, Lash & Urry 1987).

An exceptional case in this area is Australia, where the Labour Party negotiated several 'Accords' with the labour movement to restrain wages and compensate at least some workers through changes to the fiscal system. Apart from the unusually close links between the government and the labour movement (the Prime Minister is a former president of the major labour centre), the success of the Accords has been explained by the power of the Arbitration Commission. Although the commission is an autonomous body, it has chosen to support the Federal government's macro-economic policies in its arbitration awards (Dabschek & Niland 1985). Despite the unique character of the Australian industrial relations system, experience with the Accords suggests that the power of 'apolitical' regulatory agencies may be a significant variable for explaining forms of intermediation elsewhere (Dabschek 1980). Similarly, the Belgian experience, where the government imposed an incomes policy after the parties were unable to agree at the bargaining table, represents a return to policies more common in the previous two decades in several European countries (Blanpain 1987). The experience of the 1980s offers opportunities to explain the survival of corporatist systems in a period of recession that seemed to foster change in many countries.

Decentralization of collective bargaining

Apart from the declining importance of corporatist mechanisms, the level at which bipartite collective bargaining occurred became less centralized in most countries. For many countries, where wide bargaining units had served to insulate wages in the unionized sector from competition, employers introduced at least limited competition on the basis of wage costs during the 1980s. In North America, the dominant explanation for this phenomenon is a combination of management initiative and increased product market competition (Thompson & Verma 1987, Katz 1985, Jeszeck 1986).

This generalization would not extend to France, however. The Mitterrand government stimulated collective bargaining at the level of the firm in order to expand the institution generally. Despite a traditional antipathy for collective bargaining, French employers accepted this development because it gave them additional flexibility in the deployment of labour (Delamotte 1987). Thus, analyses of French industrial relations continued to stress the relationship between the government and the parties, even during the process of decentralization (see also Gourevitch et al. 1984). Again, Australia was the exception, in that the Accords centralized the structure of bargaining. The French and Australian experiences suggest that analyses of changes in bargaining structure should not neglect the role of the state, defined to include not only elected governments, but also specialized agencies with significant power in the industrial relations system.

Management and industrial relations

One of the most notable changes in industrial relations studies has been the attention given management, doubtless reflecting the initiative management has come to exercise in collective bargaining and the paucity of even basic information on the subject in most countries. In Western nations, the labour movement has traditionally been the initiator of change in patterns of employment relationships, often with strong effects in non-union sectors. Scholarship was correspondingly directed toward the labour movement or public policy rather than to the other actors. As management was seen as a source of innovation and change in the practice and results of industrial relations, research reflected this fact.

In the United States, where the ascendancy of management was especially pronounced, the shift in scholarly work was considerable. The most influential work of this genre was *The Transformation of American Industrial Relations* (Kochan *et al.* 1986, hereafter KKM). The transformation the authors analysed operated at three levels of an enterprise industrial relations system. At the top level, strategic decisions had been taken by management without much attention to industrial relations. The middle level involved the practice of collective bargaining, while the lowest level consisted of the application of policies made at the higher levels to individual workers, union officials and supervisors.

The process of transformation was based in large part on decisions at the strategic level by many employers (supported by the state) to alter fundamentally the nature of their relationship with their employees, largely away from collective bargaining as it had been practised since the 1930s. The impetus for these decisions lay in increased foreign competition faced by American manufacturers, deregulation of several sectors, and product market changes. The proposition that management (or other industrial relations actors) could exercise strategic choices in industrial relations was raised to a theoretical issue. Drawing on the literature of business policy, KKM maintained that American employers had a range of choices available on how they would carry out their industrial relations functions in a climate of severe economic pressures. For many firms, the strategic choice consisted of a variety of measures designed to eliminate or weaken their unions. Other firms worked with their unions to adapt to these pressures. Similarly, some American unions reacted in some cases by making concessions at the other two levels of their relationships in order to influence strategic labour relations decisions.

Strategic decisions resulted in changes in collective bargaining, including negotiation of wage concessions, changes in pay systems, withdrawal from employer associations, and the like. In the work place, management in some leading firms implemented policies designed to increase worker commitment to the firm (and its values) drawn from the non-union sector. These factors in turn influenced collective bargaining in the middle level and were seen to be leading to the end of the adversarial style of collective bargaining that traditionally characterized US industrial relations.

A parallel body of work has been under way in Britain. Separate studies of the Post Office (Batstone *et al.* 1984) and British Rail (Ferner 1985) examined the issue of 'management strategy' in industrial relations, drawing heavily on the labour process literature. This work was able to link management strategy in labour relations to a broader strategy for the enterprises. Though faced with both political and economic constraints, management exercised choice in the selection of measures to improve labour productivity and alter the nature of the service provided. A study of four British companies found that structures for strategic industrial relations decisions had become more centralized in the 1980s, while management had attempted to keep bargaining and operational decisions on a decentralized basis to reinforce a narrow reference area for unions in the work place (Kinnie 1985).

Application of the strategic choice model in North America has created difficulties, largely arising from the need to identify the range of feasible alternatives open to an actor. Thus, Lewin (1987) argued forcefully that management had reacted to environmental conditions in the 1980s in much the same way as it had in earlier periods, so that one could not attribute to their decisions the major change in policy implied by the term strategic choice. British scholars (Marginson *et al.* 1988) reached similar conclusions. Moreover, drawing upon Canadian data, Verma & Thompson (1989) pointed out that, despite many similarities in the two industrial relations systems, Canadian managers followed policies quite different from those of their American counterparts. Since a strategic choice is by definition a decision to change the fundamental nature of the labour–management relationship (Kochan *et al.* 1984), most Canadian managers presumably have made no strategic choices in industrial relations in recent years.

For management, the theory of strategic choice operates at the company or industry levels, but it may also explain in general terms the behaviour of management in Europe, Australasia and North America. It leaves open the issue raised by the current British government, which clearly wishes to withdraw from the corporatist systems of recognition. Will employers take the offensive against labour if they conclude that the new balance of power is permanent as their American counterparts seem to have done? An alternate proposition would be that employers, faced with relatively weak unions, may prefer to attain compliance, or perhaps even support, in the implementation of their policies through a union or works council dominated by unions rather than reverting to a unilateralist position.

The Canadian experience may be typical of that of most developed nations. In West Germany and the United Kingdom, for instance, management generally has been a moderating influence in industrial relations, usually resisting government pressures for rather dramatic change (Jacobi 1985, Brown 1985).

In Australia, a survey of managers revealed substantial support for the existing system of labour relations based on arbitration (Niland & Turner 1985). When government has imposed change favouring their bargaining position, employers have accepted the advantage proffered, but, presumably looking to a long-term relationship with their unions, have avoided initiating fundamental changes outside of the existing industrial relations framework.

A major theoretical proposition linking managerial behaviour in different national settings is Adams (1981). According to this statement, employers initially were hostile to unionism everywhere. In Europe, where unions formed part of a broad social movement, labour was able to exert political pressure to force general recognition from employers, though not at all levels of the industrial relations system. American unions opted to rely on economic pressure, so they were never able to gain the political strength necessary to win comprehensive recognition. However, Canadian unions were able to rely on the political support of a labour-backed political party to achieve greater degrees of recognition than was possible for their US counterparts.

Levels of collective bargaining

Changes in bargaining structure have stimulated the use of a multi-level framework for analysing industrial relations. Many scholars in recent years have conducted their analyses at one of the three levels, noted above, and a few have explored the relationship among them. Extensive surveys conducted in Britain produced a rich body of material on the management of industrial relations. This work examined the responsibilities of different organizational levels for industrial relations decisions, testing theoretical propositions based on the centralization of authority within the firm (Marginson *et al.* 1988). The demise of industry-wide bargaining in the American steel industry was accompanied by significant changes at the strategic and work-place levels, including shifts in product mixes that affected industrial relations (Kalwa 1987). In Australia, an examination of the relationship between the national Accords, in which employers were the junior partners, and industrial relations in the work place showed that management achieved the introduction of technological change, reduction in union jurisdictional boundaries and the like at the level of the firm or work place because of the climate the Accords created (Frenkel 1988).

Another development in collective bargaining that attracted scholarly attention was the weakening of employer associations, part of an international trend to the decentralization of bargaining. A basic source of information on employer associations in a number of developed countries was Windmuller & Gladstone (1984). Although rich in theoretical insights, the book did not attempt to formulate a general theory to explain the rise or demise of employer associations in the national context. Examining the Australian experience, Plowman (1988) found that employer associations had little influence on the structure of bargaining. The state was a more powerful factor in that regard.

A more ambitious theoretical statement arose from a comparative study of employer associations in Britain, Italy, France, and West Germany. The dominant consideration in the rise (or decline) of employer associations was the nature of the 'trade union challenge', i.e. the nature of union bargaining demands and structure of the national labour movement. Less important were factors such as corporate concentration or market structures. Thus, union structure might be as important a determinant of bargaining structure as management organization (Sisson 1987, Fulcher 1988).

Implications for theory and methodology

As collective bargaining became more decentralized, the attention of scholars tended to shift to the level of the firm or work place, away from individual-based variables or broad generalizations about social conditions. In the 1970s US research, for instance, extensively utilized deductive models and quantitative analysis contrary to an IR tradition of fact-gathering and induction (Capelli 1985). In the following decade, the pendulum swung back somewhat. Case-studies re-emerged from disfavour to become a more significant research tool. Much of the KKM work, for instance, was essentially inductive, based on a series of case studies, often relying on relatively small data sets. Studies of management policy, in particular, seem to lend themselves to that methodology and one can expect more attention to be paid to systems at the level of the firm or plant in future research (see Koshiro 1983).

From a methodological point of view, the new US literature resembles recent British and Australian work, with emphasis on data collection and inductive analysis, more than US research of the previous decade. Perhaps one of the enduring contributions of industrial relations research of this decade will be a blending of methodologies in the same projects.

Alternatives to collective bargaining

Inevitably, the decline in the importance of collective bargaining sparked searches for alternatives to the traditional system of collective bargaining in a particular society. These proposals take many different forms. In Europe, the absence of a formal trade union presence in the work place stimulated the creation of works councils to act as consultative bodies supplementary to collective bargaining which is conducted at corporate or industrial levels. In some countries, there is a requirement that employees be represented on corporate boards of directors. In North America, where unions were strongly entrenched in the work place, many participation plans were management-initiated substitutes for collective bargaining in non-union settings. In Japan, employers often sponsor participation systems to capitalize on union weakness (Park 1984).

As Lansbury & Davis (in press) point out, the vocabulary in public debates over democratization of the employment relationship reflects these competing tendencies. Unions and their political and intellectual supporters promote 'industrial democracy' mechanisms to ensure that management shares some of its power with employees, a popular notion in postwar Europe, for instance. Managers are more likely to advocate 'employee participation' programmes as a means of encouraging loyalty to the firm, higher productivity and the like, objectives which were more in vogue in the 1980s. Industrial democracy usually is supported by statute or other public policy, while employee participation operates independently of any legal support. This distinction usefully highlights some of the differences in mechanisms under discussion in the 1980s, as well as raising theoretical issues about the coexistence of participation or democracy and collective bargaining.

The emergence of 'employee involvement' plans in US unionized firms added a new dimension to research on participation. The reaction of the labour movement to these management initiatives ranged from outright opposition to enthusiastic support. In a conservative political climate legal support for these programmes is scarcely discussed. Cutcher-Gersenfeld *et al.* (in press) hypothesized that employee involvement plans that rely on union support would be more difficult to establish, but are likely to survive longer than systems established unilaterally by management. Partial support for this hypothesis was found in one study of a programme to which the union was neutral. Workers who volunteered were less active in the union than non-volunteers, but at the same time wanted more participation by their union (Verma & McKersie 1987).

The Japanese experience raises additional issues. A debate similar to that in North America on the implications of consultation without legal regulation has arisen. One view holds that consultation further weakens a labour movement already enfeebled in the work place (Tokunaga 1983). Alternatively, quality of working life programmes can be seen as a force for more benign conditions for workers (Koshiro 1983). However, labour–management consultation appears to be growing in the unionized sector of the economy at the level of the enterprise and on a national level on a tripartite basis (Taira & Levine 1985). Because of the enterprise orientation of labour markets and union structures in that country, employers feel free to provide sensitive information to union leaders serving on consultative bodies. Could consultation, currently a supplement to collective bargaining, supplant formal negotiations?

In West Germany, the relative importance of centralized wage negotiation has declined in the face of increasing bargaining activities by works councils, which have assumed a stronger role in the negotiation of protection against technological change, flexible working time and the like (Streeck 1987). Similarly, consultation seems to be increasing in Great Britain, where employer desires for productivity improvement have been met by worker concerns about job security (Windmuller 1987). There is no statutory requirement for participation, though the current government favours consultation over collective bargaining. Given the growing decentralization of collective bargaining in Great Britain, the theoretical implications for systems of consultation are that the maintenance of the distinction between bargaining activities and consultation depends on conducting these activities at different levels of the industrial relations system. Thus bargaining could conflict with consultation in Britain, so that only one institution survives, or that different jurisdictions are established.

Australian national politics have been dominated by the Labour Party, so discussion of industrial democracy is common. However, the employer community favours employee participation, and the labour movement is reluctant to support changes that could undermine its monopoly of representation in the labour force. In turbulent economic times, the Labour Party has been unwilling to impose any arrangements to alter the distribution of authority in the work place without greater consensus (Lansbury & Davis in press). Theory indicates that the best opportunities for participation will be at the level of the firm or industry, but such plans would have to deal with the arbitration tribunals that are so central to Australian industrial relations.

Conclusions

Changes in industrial relations described here have disturbed many scholars, who hold the pluralistic values that support collective bargaining and other formal systems of employee representation. In some nations, the size and prosperity of the profession are linked with the decline in bilateral industrial relations processes. Whatever their personal sentiments or stake in these developments, industrial relations scholars have analysed the processes of change and developed a substantial body of data and theory to explain them. In the neo-conservative vocabulary of this period, the study of industrial relations may be becoming smaller, but more robust.

References

Adams, Roy J. 1988. Desperately seeking industrial relations theory. *International Journal of Comparative Labour Law, and Industrial Relations* 4, 1, Spring, 1–10.

Adams, Roy J. 1985. Industrial relations and the economic crisis: Canada moves toward Europe. In *Industrial Relations in a Decade of Economic Change*, H. Juris, M. Thompson & W. Daniels (eds), 115–50. Madison, Wisc.: Industrial Relations Research Association.

Adams, Roy J. 1981. A theory of employer attitudes and behaviour trade unions in Western Europe and North America. In *Management Under Differing Value Systems*, G. Dlugos & K. Weiermair (eds), 275–93. Berlin: de Gruyter.

Audet, Michel & Viateur Larouche 1988. Paradigmes, écoles de pensée et théories en relations industrielles. *Relations Industrielles* 43, 1, 3–31.

Batstone, Eric, Anthony Ferner & Michael Terry 1984. *Consent and Efficiency: Labour Relations and Management Strategy in the State Enterprise*. Oxford: Blackwell.

Beaumont, Philip B. 1988. The role of the state in industrial relations: a European perspective. Presented at the First Industrial Relations Congress of the Americas, Quebec, Canada.

Blanpain, R. 1987. Belgium. In *Collective Bargaining in Industrialized Market Economies: A Reappraisal*, International Labour Office, 177–87. Geneva: International Labour Office.

Brown, William 1983. The impact of high unemployment on bargaining structure. *Journal of Industrial Relations* 25, 2, June, 132–9.

Brown, William 1985. The effect of recent changes in the world economy on British industrial relations. In *Industrial Relations in a Decade of Economic Change*, H. Juris, M. Thompson & W. Daniels (eds), 151–76. Madison, Wisc.: Industrial Relations Research Association.

Caire, Guy 1987. France. In *Collective Bargaining in Industrialized Market Economies: A Reappraisal*, International Labour Office, 191–208. Geneva: International Labour Office.

Capelli, Peter 1985. Theory construction in industrial relations and some implications for research. *Industrial Relations* 24, 1, Winter, 90–112.

Cutcher–Gersenfeld, Joel, Thomas A. Kochan & Anil Verma in press. Recent developments in U.S. employee involvement initiatives. In *Advances in Industrial and Labor Relations*. Vol. 5.

Dabschek, Braham 1980. The Australian system of industrial relations: an analytical model. *Journal of Industrial Relations* 22, 3, June, 196–218.

Dabschek, Braham & John Niland 1985. Australian industrial relations and the shift to centralism. In *Industrial Relations in a Decade of Economic*

Change, H. Juris, M. Thompson & W. Daniels (eds). Madison, Wisc.: Industrial Relaitons Research Association.

Delamotte, Yves 1987. Industrial relations: agenda for change: France. Prepared for the Working Party on Industrial Relations, Organization for Economic Co–operation and Development, Paris, September.

Edwards, R. & M. Podgursky 1986. The unravelling accord: American unions in crisis. In *Unions in Crisis and Beyond*, R. Edwards, P. Garonna & F. Todtling (eds), 14–60. London: Auburn House.

Ferner, Anthony 1985. Political constraints and management strategies: the case of working practices in British Rail. *British Journal of Industrial Relations* **XXXIII**, 1, March, 47–70.

Frenkel, Stephen J. 1988. Australian employers in the shadow of the labor accords. *Industrial Relations* **27**, 2, Spring, 166–79.

Fulcher, James 1988. On the explanation of industrial relations diversity: labour movements, employers and the state in Britain and Sweden. *British Journal of Industrial Relations* **26**, 2, July, 246–74.

Goldthorpe, John (ed.) 1984. *Order and Conflict in Contemporary Capitalism*. Oxford: Clarendon.

Gospel, Howard F. 1983. New managerial approaches to industrial relations: major paradigms and historical perspective. *Journal of Industrial Relations* **25**, 1, June, 162–76.

Gourevitch, Peter, Andrew Martin, George Ross, Christopher Allen, Stephen Bornstein & Andrei Markovits 1984. *Unions and Economic Crisis: Britain, West Germany and Sweden*. London: Allen & Unwin.

Heneman, Jr, Herbert G. 1969. Toward a general conceptual system of industrial relations: how do we get there? In *Essays in Industrial Relations Theory*, Gerald G. Somers (ed.), 3–24. Ames, Ia: Iowa State University Press.

Jacobi, Otto 1985. World economic changes and industrial relations in the Federal Republic of Germany. In *Industrial Relations in a Decade of Economic Change*, H. Juris, M. Thompson & W. Daniels (eds), 211–46. Madison, Wisc.: Industrial Relations Research Association.

Jeszeck, Charles 1986. Structural change in collective bargaining: the United States tire industry. *Industrial Relations* **25**, 3, Fall, 229–47.

Juris, Hervey, Mark Thompson & Wilbur Daniels 1985. *Industrial Relations in a Decade of Economic Change*. Madison, Wisc.: Industrial Relations Research Association.

Kalwa, Richard W. [1986] 1987. Collective bargaining in steel: a strategic perspective. *Proceedings of the 39th Annual Meeting of the Industrial Relations Research Association*, 313–19. Madison, Wisc.: Industrial Relations Research Association.

Katz, Harry C. 1985. *Shifting Gears: Changing Labor Relations in the U.S. Automobile Industry*. Cambridge, Mass.: MIT Press.

Kinnie, N. J. 1985. Changing management strategies in industrial relations. *Industrial Relations Journal* **16**, 4, Winter, 17–24.

Kirkbride, P. S. 1985. The concept of power: a lacuna in industrial relations theory? *Journal of Industrial Relations* **27**, 3, September, 265–82.

Kochan, Thomas A., Harry C. Katz & Robert B. McKersie 1986. *The Transformation of American Industrial Relations*. New York: Basic Books.

Kochan, Thomas A., Robert B. McKersie & Peter Capelli 1984. Strategic choice and industrial relations theory. *Industrial Relations* **23**, Winter, 16–39.

Koshiro, Kazutochi 1983. The quality of working life in Japanese factories. In *Contemporary Industrial Relations in Japan*, Taishiro Shirai (ed.), 63–88. Madison, Wisc.: University of Wisconsin Press.

Kumar, Pradeep, Mary Lou Coates & David Arrowsmith 1988. *The Current Industrial Relations Scene in Canada, 1988*. Kingston, Ont.: Industrial Relations Centre, Queen's University.

Lansbury, Russell and Edward M. Davis in press. Employee involvement and workers' participation in management – the Australian experience. *Advances in Industrial and Labor Relations*. Vol. 5.

Larouche, Viateur & Esther Déom 1984. L'approche systemique en relations industrielles. *Relations Industrielles* **39**, 1, 114–45.

Lash, Scott 1985. The end of neo-corporatism? The breakdown of centralized bargaining in Sweden. *British Journal of Industrial Relations* **XXIII**, 2, July, 215–39.

Lash, Scott & John Urry 1987. *The End of Organized Capitalism*. London: Polity.

Lewin, David 1987. Industrial relations as a strategic variable. In *Human Resources and the Performance of the Firm*, Morris M. Kleiner, Richard N. Block, Myron Roomkin & Sidney W. Salsburg (eds), 1–42. Madison, Wisc.: Industrial Relations Research Association.

Marginson, Paul, P. K. Edwards, John Purcell & Keith Sisson 1988. What do corporate offices really do? *British Journal of Industrial Relations* **XXVI**, 2, July, 229–45.

Niland, John & Dennis Turner 1985. *Control, Consensus or Chaos? Managers and Industrial Relations Reform*. Sydney: Allen & Unwin.

Park, S. J. 1984. Labour-management consultation as a Japanese type of participation. In *Industrial Relations in Transition: The Case of Japan and the Federal Republic of Germany*, Shigeyoshi Tokunaga & Joachim Bergman (eds), 153–67. Tokyo: University of Tokyo Press.

Plowman, David 1988. Employer associations and bargaining structures: an Australian perspective. *British Journal of Industrial Relations* **XXVI**, 3, November, 371–96.

Poole, Michael 1988. Industrial relations theory and managerial strategies. *International Journal of Comparative Labour Law and Industrial Relations* **IV**, 11–24.

Reshef, Yonatan & Alan I. Murray 1988. Toward a neo-institutionalist approach in industrial relations. *British Journal of Industrial Relations* **XXVI**, 1, March, 85–98.

Shirom, Arie 1985. The labour relations system: a proposed conceptual framework. *Relations Industrielles* **40**, 2, 303–23.

Sisson, Keith 1987. *The Management of Collective Bargaining: An International Comparison*. Oxford: Blackwell.

Streeck, Wolfgang 1987. Industrial relations: agenda for change: the Federal Republic of Germany. Organization for Economic Co-operation and Development, Working Party on Industrial Relations.

Taira, Koji & Solomon B. Levine 1985. Japan's industrial relations: a social compact emerges. In *Industrial Relations in a Decade of Economic Change*, H. Juris, M. Thompson & W. Daniels (eds), 247–300. Madison, Wisc.: Industrial Relations Research Association.

Thompson, Mark & Hervey Juris 1985. The response of industrial relations to economic change. In *Industrial Relations in a Decade of Economic Change*, H. Juris, M. Thompson & W. Daniels (eds), 383–407. Madison, Wisc.: Industrial Relations Research Association.

Thompson, Mark & Anil Verma 1987. Management strategies in the 1980's: the Canadian experience. Presented to the Second European Regional Congress, International Industrial Relations Association, Herzlia, Israel.

Tokunaga, Shigeyoshi 1983. A Marxist interpretation of Japanese industrial relations with special reference to large private enterprises. In *Contemporary Industrial Relations in Japan*, Taishiro Shirai (ed.), 313–30. Madison, Wisc.: University of Wisconsin Press.

Turnbull, Peter J. 1988. The economic theory of trade union behaviour: a critique. *British Journal of Industrial Relations* **XXVI**, 1, March, 99–118.

Verma, Anil & Robert B. McKersie 1987. Employee involvement: the implications of non-involvement by unions. *Industrial and Labor Relations Review* **40**, 4, July, 556–68.

Verma, Anil & Mark Thompson 1989. Managerial strategies in Canada and the United States in the 1980s. *Proceedings of the 41st Annual Meeting of the Industrial Relations Research Association, December 1988*. Madison, Wisc.: Industrial Relations Research Association.

Windmuller, John P. 1987. Comparative study of methods and practices. In *Collective Bargaining in Industrialized Market Economies: A Reappraisal*, International Labour Office, 3–158. Geneva: International Labour Office.

Windmuller, John P. & Alan Gladstone 1984. *Employer Associations and Industrial Relations: A Comparative Study*. Oxford: Clarendon.

8 Recent trends in industrial relations research and theory in developing countries

TAYO FASHOYIN

Introduction

A review of industrial relations research in developing countries is made difficult by the definitional problem of what falls within the horizons of industrial relations. In many countries industrial relations, as known in Western democracies, do not really exist, either because the industrial base is weak or poor, or because of the reluctance of the ruling elite to allow the existence of strong and independent union movements.

This problem apart, much of the available research on developing countries focuses on the wider economic and social context of industrial relations, while a little focuses more exclusively on the narrower plane of union–management relations. In the latter case, a good number of the volumes that have appeared in recent years (e.g. Damachi *et al.* 1979, on Africa) contain research studies on national industrial relations systems. Studies of this kind are not comparative in the real sense of the term. Exceptions to this approach are the fully comparative studies by Schregle (1982) on southern Asia and Córdova (1984) on Latin America. Other earlier works are Roberts & Bellecombe (1967) and Meynaud & Saleh-Bey (1967), both on Africa.

Another point of note is the dramatic decline in the pace of research by Western authors since the 1970s. Except for the International Labour Office (ILO) which, by constitution, is committed to research in all member states, there have been comparatively few Western research works on developing countries. I make this remark, bearing in mind the keen interest shown in the developing countries and the publication of such highly useful studies as Kerr *et al.* (1960), Kassalow (1963 and 1969), Sturmthal & Scoville (1973), Galenson (1959 and 1962), Roberts (1964), and Millen (1963) all of which appeared in the pre- and post-independence period of the 1960s and 1970s.

Scoville (1982) offers partial statistical evidence on the declining trend in comparative research and publication in the industrially advanced countries. He shows that during the period 1955–72, 1525 pages in the three leading scholarly US journals were devoted to comparative research, in contrast to 1099 pages during 1973–8. He suggested that industrial relations issues, particularly in the developing countries, important though they may be, were no longer challenging to upcoming and younger American researchers. Happily, an increasing number of serious scholars in the developing countries have risen to the challenge and it is encouraging to observe the impressive list of research studies by them.

In what follows, I will review five subject areas: the labour movement, collective bargaining, labour markets, the role of government, and industrial conflict. My choice of the five thematic areas, although somewhat subjective and arbitrary, nevertheless represents the mainstream of industrial relations research. While the focus is on Africa, Asia and Latin America, the review obviously does not present an equitable balance among the three geographical regions.

The labour movement

The research of the post-independence period was strongly influenced by the work of the Interuniversity Study of Labour Problems in Economic Development (Kerr *et al.* 1960).

This huge project sponsored more than 40 specific studies in 35 countries. A major focus of this work and other studies stimulated by it was on the role of trade unions in the independence struggle. Research suggested that unions in developing countries had a limited economic impact but that they played an important political role. Researchers were particularly concerned with the relationship between unions and nationalist movements (see e.g. Kerr *et al.* 1960 and Millen 1963).

Gladstone (1980) explained this concern as follows:

The real or presumed role of trade unions in the independence movements and the identification of prominent trade union
leaders with those movements is of importance because of their
effects in shaping and developing the nature of trade unions
after independence, and concomitantly the relations between the
unions, political parties and governments. (p. 51)

After independence, political activity continued to be high on
union agendas (Busch 1980) and the focus of research shifted to
union–state relations. In countries where their attention was not
focused on the fight against neo-colonial forces, unions typically
engaged in seeking a voice in national economic (and sometimes
political) decision-making (Ananaba 1979). In countries where they
were not so free their political activity centred on achieving autonomy
for themselves.

Martens (1979) records that in the French-speaking African countries a large number of labour leaders attained political positions
in either the party or government. In Singapore the ruling party
employed a divide-and-rule strategy by supporting a friendly faction
until it had succeeded in neutralizing an unfriendly one (Pang
& Cheng 1978). Amjad & Mahmood (1982), writing on Pakistan,
observed that while the government avoided the Singapore strategy, it favoured the emergence of an acceptable union leadership.
In Brazil and Argentina, successive military dictatorships trampled
workers' rights and employed a variety of repressive measures to
undermine the labour movement (Munck 1987).

Studies have, however, cautioned that these state strategies of
harnessing and subordinating unions often have been unstable.
The Ghanaian case is illustrative. When the general-secretary of the
Trades Union Congress (TUC) (the country's only union centre)
became a functionary of Nkrumah's ruling Convention People's
Party (CPP), union leaders at the national and enterprise levels
ignored the TUC and created a new centre of power within their
unions (Damachi 1974).

A good number of class-oriented studies on working class forma-
tions and their relationship with the government have also emerged.
Notable works are Sandbrook & Cohen (1975) which focused on
Africa, Boyd *et al.* (1987), and Southall (1987 and 1988). The latter two contain contributions across continental boundaries. Many
national studies, such as Sandbrook's work on Kenya, have also
appeared.

One important concept which has developed from this research is the 'labour aristocracy' thesis put forth by Arrighi & Saul (1968). It argues that the unionized workers in urban African countries constitute a privileged minority whose economic and social conditions have been enhanced at the expense of the vast majority of rural dwellers and the urban poor in the informal sector. This is a good thesis, which should evoke considerably more debate than it has received (Peace 1979).

Another focus of Marxist research has been corporatism. At one end of the spectrum, corporatism is defined as institutionized cooperation between independent interest groups and the state in economic policy formulation and implementation (Collier & Collier 1979). At the other end, corporatism presumes a political coalition of institutions subordinate to the will of the state (Pepel & Tsunekawa 1979). The formal objective of corporatist arrangements is the achievement of tripartite (labour–management–government) consensus regarding economic and social policy. While various forms exist in the developing world, available evidence suggests that none of them has achieved resounding success in attaining its goals (Collier 1979). Because of their focus on labour–management conflict as a consequence of class struggle, Marxist researchers have generally neglected the actual processes of industrial relations.

The book by Kassalow & Damachi (1978) is a fairly recent and important contribution to the research on trade unions in developing countries. Kassalow regards this volume as providing 'a useful opportunity to make a retrospective foray into [existing] literature and, at the same time, to clarify some present trends and prospects for trade unionism in new countries' (p.6). In particular, the contributions by Damachi on Ghana, Pang and Cheng on Singapore, Ramos on the Philippines, and Ogle on Korea offer new insights and indicate the need to reconsider arguments developed in earlier decades (see e.g. Galenson 1959, Galenson 1962 and Millen 1963). These studies suggest that future research should focus on the gains or inroads made by unions in national economic and social policy formulation.

Collective bargaining

Generally, research on collective bargaining in developing countries focuses on the extent, nature, scope and structure of bargaining.

The studies of the recent period reveal that collective bargaining has become a well-accepted means of regulating employment conditions in Asia (Schregle 1982), Africa (Damachi *et al.* 1979), and Latin America (Córdova 1980a and 1984). These studies document a transition away from the pervasive state intervention of the early independence period to the current period when the parties are assuming greater direct responsibility for establishing employment conditions. There are, however, exceptions to this general trend especially in the public sector.

In Latin America, Córdova's (1980a) study reveals an increasing use of autonomous bargaining machinery and a noticeable departure from interventionist models. However, he cautions that the increasing autonomy might run counter to government commitment to deal with contemporary economic difficulties. A similar conclusion would be true of African countries which are faced with the problem of implementing externally prescribed (e.g. World Bank, IMF) structural adjustment measures to deal with intractable economic problems (Fashoyin & Damachi 1988).

What has emerged from the research is the concept of 'tripartism' in bargaining. Although this is neither a new concept nor a generally accepted principle, nevertheless, it describes the negotiations that are taking place in many developing Asian countries (Schregle 1982). In Africa, the tripartite agreements in Kenya, which were signed in the 1970s, demonstrated the commitment of the three parties to deal genuinely with industrial relations problems (Stewart 1979). Where functional institutions for regulating incomes, such as incomes policy boards and committees, exist, tripartism is usually the main means of regulating wages, particularly at the macro level.

Research has also revealed the ups and downs in collective bargaining in a number of countries. In Korea, Bognanno & Kim (1982) found that the machinery was acquiring some stability when the government, fearing a loss of control, severely restricted its use in the early 1980s. For much the same reason, in many countries of Africa (Ubeku 1983), Asia (Schregle 1982) and Latin America (Córdova 1980b), collective bargaining has gained only a weak foothold in the public sector. Legislative restrictions have not, however, always been successful in keeping public employees quiescent. In many countries they have formed unions in order to influence their conditions of work despite legal constraints on formal negotiations. Collective bargaining has gained impetus especially in autonomous public sector institutions.

While the foregoing evidence shows significant differences in the use of collective bargaining in developing countries, the general trend is towards increasing use of the machinery, whether bilateral or tripartite.

Research on collective bargaining in developing countries has generally neglected the actual negotiation process and the behavioural propensities of the negotiators. The vast majority of studies to date (e.g. Schregle 1982, Córdova 1980b, Gray 1980, and Muir & Brown 1978), focus on macro aspects of the subject. There are only a few studies, such as Smock (1969), which have looked at bargaining in specific union–management relationships. There is therefore a lot to be done, with emphasis on case studies in specific industries and on behavioural issues in negotiations.

Within the broad subject of labour–management relations a few studies have examined the subject of workers' participation. The thrust of this research is on the extent to which the parties deal with each other, beyond the confines of collective bargaining, in their day-to-day relationship. This literature suggests that participation has not generally been an effective vehicle of worker representation and prospects for the future are not particularly good. In particular there remains strong employer resistance to participation even among large multinational and indigenous companies that have accepted collective bargaining. Although governments in some countries (e.g. India and Pakistan) have made legislative provisions in support of participation, implementation has been half-hearted. Trade union leaders are often ambivalent, especially if they expect participation to undercut their influence and the control of the union.

The Latin American experience, as recorded by Córdova (1980a), is indicative of the general situation in the developing countries. He remarked:

> There has, moreover, been some resistance to the establishment of joint councils or other bodies designed to foster collaboration or deal with subjects of mutual interest. Certain legislative experiments relating to self-management (Argentina), co-determination (Chile) or labour committees (Peru) have been abandoned, substantially altered or deprived of their most striking participatory features. (p. 234)

In African countries joint consultative machinery exists but, for the most part, it is used for collective bargaining purposes. Also, tripartite bodies on broader economic and social issues exist but, as indicated above, they are often under-utilized or bypassed altogether. Exceptions to this were the developments of the 1980s when difficult economic conditions induced both sides of industry in several nations to collaborate in dealing with the problems of low-capacity utilization, redundancy and job security (Fashoyin 1986a). These problems have drawn labour and management into closer co-operation for mutual survival, although it is unclear whether this is a transient phase or the beginning of a deep-seated appreciation of the mutuality of their interest in the undertaking. If the trend towards co-operation persists, it may arouse academic interest in developing a framework of analysis based on the concept of stakeholder or on the mutuality of the interests of workers and employers.

Labour markets

I propose to treat only two topics under this fairly extensive subject area. These are incomes policy and employment. I chose the former because it represents one subject which suddenly generated research interest and then dramatically evaporated, and the latter because it remains an area of enduring research interest.

Wage issues have attracted considerable research attention for some time (see e.g. Warren 1966 and Berg 1969). Since the mid-1960s work in this area has focused largely on the widespread use by developing countries of incomes policies (although it is difficult to understand why these countries should have been using such policies in the first place). Sunkel's work on the structural basis of inflation in Latin America and on the potential of incomes policy to play an ameliorating role was particularly useful in that he developed a theoretical framework applicable to the situation in many developing nations (Sunkel 1958).

Other highly useful pieces of research on this subject are Kirkpatrick & Nixson (1976), Thorp (1971), and Onitiri & Awosika (1982). These studies have considerable theoretical appeal. They emphasize that inflation in developing countries has deep-rooted causes and that policies designed to control prices must keep in mind the inevitable consequences which they have for the overall development process.

Effective institutional mechanisms for implementing incomes policy measures are uncommon in developing countries and incomes policies often have distorted existing income relationships. They also have failed regularly to address seriously such problems as income redistribution, maladjustment in the labour market, and the problem of balance of payments. Fashoyin (1986b), Routh (1969), Fry (1979), Killick (1973), and Mohammed-Taha (1979) are representative authors of country studies that have argued the futility of controlling incomes in African countries.

Employment has received impressive attention in academic research since independence. The ILO has been the main supporter of studies which have explored means of achieving the maximum level of employment consistent with the development effort. Comprehensive studies on Kenya (1972), the Philippines (1974), and Ceylon (1971) are representative of a number of serious scholarly national works which have emerged from the ILO's massive World Employment Programme.

In the sub-area of labour markets, the volumes by Sethuraman (1981) and Kannappan (1977) are highly useful compilations of research on urban labour markets. In this area also are Scoville (1974) and Fapohunda *et al.* (1978). These studies have made useful contributions to the growing knowledge of the functioning of urban labour markets and the crucial role of the informal sector. They have documented the segmented nature of these markets in most developing nations with typically a small number of workers having relatively secure jobs with large corporations and government bureaucracies while the majority survive on insecure casual employment.

A lot of work is still needed especially on the nature and functioning of the underground economy. Findings from such studies might provide a better and more realistic policy direction. Also, given the increasing importance of the informal sector as a source of employment for those who lose their jobs in the formal sector, there is need for more research on the nature of the informal sector in the 1990s. Such research should focus, among others, on the linkages between the formal and informal sectors, and the employment processes in the latter (Harriss *et al.* 1989).

The role of government

Research on the role of government in industrial relations in developing countries has been quite extensive. In the post-independence period, research has focused less on abstentionist and voluntarist policies and more on explanations and consequences of increased interventionist policies.

In general, government intervention became commonplace after independence. Myers & Kannappan (1970) argue that the Indian government began to take an active role in industrial relations even before independence. After independence, as the country faced the problems of a new nation and a postwar labour outburst, public policy altered in favour of dramatically increased control.

The reason for the attention of researchers on this subject goes beyond the fact that governments are usually the major employers. Additionally, in quite a large number of countries, the state has assumed leadership in both the political and economic spheres. In such countries as the United Republic of Tanzania and the Sudan, for example, the commitment to socialist policies led to the nationalization of virtually all economic sectors. Even in countries that have followed capitalist development paths, such as Brazil and Nigeria, the public sector is quite large. Therefore, the interest and involvement of governments in industrial relations matters beyond the limit of legislation and procedures must be explained in part by the active involvement of government in business enterprises.

Apart from this, there is the real or imagined threat which unions pose to the ruling elite. In countries where there is political instability, and a large number of developing countries fall into this category, unions are often seen as being a potential alternative to the ruling party (Ananaba 1979). In response, several countries have developed strategies to deal with the presumed threat of trade unions.

One line of research, undertaken by industrial relations pluralists, has centred on the concern of governments for the promotion of economic growth and development in an atmosphere of relative industrial peace, with the unions playing an important role. This framework raised considerable academic debate in the 1950s and 1960s and, although not much has been written on it in the 1970s and 1980s, I am not convinced either that the debate has ended or that the issues in dispute will become any less important in the 1990s.

The debate centres on the consumptionist and productionist theses (see Kassalow 1963 and 1969, Galenson 1959 and 1962, and Damachi 1974, for a summary of both theses). One view sees the unions as consumptionist institutions concerned with bread-and-butter issues; in short, their concern is with the sectoral interests of their members. The other view sees unions as a vehicle for stimulating productivity within a productionist framework in which sectoral interests are subordinated (perhaps temporarily) to national interests of increased productivity and moderation in wage demands.

As I have argued elsewhere (Fashoyin 1986c), both positions are misleading because they construct a narrow picture of what unions are, what they do, and how they do it. There is hardly any serious union in a developing country that can entirely pursue the self-interest of its members and remain oblivious to its environment and the socioeconomic structure of production.

Yet, the latter argument, i.e. the productionist thesis, has become the one used by the ruling elite to interfere with industrial relations institutions. Gladstone (1980) and Essenberg (1985) document the varying forms of intervention. Many countries permit only a single trade union centre which is often allied with the ruling political party. Commonly, as noted above, legislative measures have been taken to restrict the freedom of unions in using bargaining machinery, striking, or asserting their rights in other ways.

The 1980s saw a global expansion of political democracy. If that trend continues into the 1990s one might expect a relaxation of state control of industrial relations institutions and processes and greater freedom for trade unions.

Industrial conflict

Industrial conflict in developing countries, in which the level of industrialization is generally low, often has more complex dimensions than does 'pure' industrial conflict. In addition to conflict over conditions of work there are conflicts of interest, of personality and so forth in political and economic leadership. Western observers might dismiss these types as superficial, but it is often the case in developing countries that industrial disputes in the work place are connected to broader social forces rather than being 'purely' over job interests.

Unfortunately, research on this topic has not provided a convincing theoretical analysis of the dimensions and shape of industrial conflict. Some Marxist-oriented studies have appeared (e.g. Waterman 1976), but they follow the familiar class arguments without explaining the actual situations in work places.

Research on strikes has given due attention to the issue of the right to strike in various countries. Hardly is there a country where the right to strike has not been tampered with. Where there is no outright ban on strikes, strict conditions are laid down for legal strikes to occur. According to Jecchinis's (1978) study on Greece, a constitutional provision was made against 'any strike motivated by political or other aims alien to the material and moral interests of the worker'.

Jackson (1979) wrote on the disappearance of strikes in the United Republic of Tanzania after legal impediments were placed on the right to strike. Yet other writers, such as Bienefeld (1979) and Shivji (1976), have contradicted Jackson by arguing that acquiescence has only changed the form of protest and that obedience was achieved mainly because of contradictions in national policies.

Ogle's (1978) account of disputes settlement machinery in South Korea is representative of the general research evidence across the developing world. He asserts:

Rather than continue to function as third-party mediator of disputes, the South Korean Government has become the primary actor in labour–management relations. Government now attempts to prevent the expression of conflict and, where conflict does appear, it is now the Government that claims the power to settle it. Government has usurped the responsibility, previously held by the unions and employers, of resolving conflict situations. (p. 147)

Yet, research evidence has also indicated the impotence of anti-strike laws and that restrictions have had only a moderating effect on the propensity to strike.

An overview

Based on the foregoing survey, the general conclusion is that the scope of industrial relations research in developing countries has broadened substantially since the 1950s and 1960s. More recent studies have indicated a need to go beyond the generalizations of the past to develop models of industrial relations which better reflect environmental diversity and specific national characteristics.

In the interaction between unions, employers and the state, government continues to dominate and thus the problems of government continue to attract a great deal of research attention. The state commonly sets not only the rules and procedures of labour–

management interaction but also the substantive conditions of work. Despite the continued widespread dominance of the state, independent collective bargaining, nevertheless, has made considerable progress during the past two decades.

What future is there for a more equitable or balanced tripartite relationship, especially in an era of intractable economic difficulties? It seems to me that in order to strengthen our understanding of the respective roles of the parties and of appropriate frameworks of interaction, future research should focus on micro-level studies in the areas of collective bargaining, the negotiation process, labour–management co-operation, and union leadership.

References

Amjad, R. & K. Mahmood 1982. *Industrial Relations and the Political Process in Pakistan, 1947–77.* Geneva: International Institute for Labour Studies, Research Series No. 73.

Ananaba, W. 1979. *The Trade Union Movement in Africa.* London: C. Hurst.

Arrighi, G. & J. S. Saul 1968. Socialism and economic development in tropical Africa. *Journal of Modern African Studies* **6**, 141–69.

Berg, E. J. 1969. Urban real wages and the Nigerian trade union movement 1939–60: a comment. *Economic Development and Cultural Change* **17**, July, 604–17.

Bienefeld, M.A. 1979. Trade unions, the labour process and the Tanzanian state. *Journal of Modern African Studies* **17**, 4, 553–93.

Bognanno, M. F. & S. Kim 1982. Collective bargaining in Korea. *Proceedings of the 34th Annual Meeting of the Industrial Relations Research Association, December 1981.* Madison, Wisc.: Industrial Relations Research Association.

Boyd, R. E. *et al.* (eds) 1987. *International Labour and the Third World. The Making of a New Working Class.* London: Gower.

Busch, G. K. 1980. *Political Currents in the International Trade Union Movement.* Vol. 2: *The Third World.* London: Economist Intelligence Unit, Report No. 75.

Collier, David, (ed.) 1979. *The New Authoritarianism in Latin America.* Princeton, NJ: Princeton University Press.

Collier, R. B. & David Collier 1979. Inducements versus constraints: disagregating corporatism'. *The American Political Science Review* **73**, 4, 967–86.

Córdova, E. 1980a. Collective labour relations in Latin America: a reappraisal. *Labour and Society* **5**, 227–42.

Córdova, E. 1980b. Labour relations in the public service in Latin America. *International Labour Review* **119**, 5, 579–94.

Córdova, E. 1984. *Industrial Relations in Latin America.* New York: Praeger.

Damachi, U. G. 1974. *The Role of Trade Unions in the Development Process. With a Case Study of Ghana*. New York: Praeger.

Damachi, U. G. *et al.* (eds) 1979. *Industrial Relations in Africa*. London: Macmillan.

Edwards, E. O. (ed.) 1974. *Employment in Developing Nations*. New York: Columbia University Press.

Essenberg, B. 1985. *The Interaction of Industrial Relations and the Political Process in Selected Developing Countries of Africa and Asia. A Comparative Analysis*. Geneva: International Institute for Labour Studies, Research Series No. 81.

Fapohunda, O. J. *et al.* 1978. *Lagos: Urban Development and Employment*. Geneva: International Labour Office.

Fashoyin, Tayo 1986a. Collective bargaining challenges during economic recession. In *Contemporary Problems in Nigerian Industrial Relations*, U. G. Damachi & Tayo Fashoyin (eds). Lagos: Development Press.

Fashoyin, Tayo 1986b. *Incomes and Inflation in Nigeria*. Lagos & London: Longman.

Fashoyin, Tayo 1986c. Trade unions and economic development in Africa. *International Studies of Management and Organization* 16, 2, Summer, 59–78.

Fashoyin, Tayo & U. G. Damachi 1988. Labour relations and African development. *Nigerian Journal of Industrial Relations* 2, December.

Fry, James. 1979. *Employment and Income Distribution in the African Economy*. London: Croom Helm.

Galenson, Walter 1959. *Labor and Economic Development*. New York: John Wiley.

Galenson, Walter 1962. *Labor in Developing Countries*. Berkeley and Los Angeles, Calif.: University of California Press.

Ghai, D. *et al.* (eds) 1979. *Planning for Basic Needs in Kenya*. Geneva: International Labour Office.

Gladstone, Alan 1980. Trade unions, growth and development. *Labour and Society* 5, 1, January, 49–68.

Gray, P. S. 1980. Collective bargaining in Ghana. *Industrial Relations* 19, 2, Spring, 175–91.

Harriss, I., K. P. Kannan & G. Rodgers 1989. *Urban Labour Markets Structure and Job Access in India: A Study of Coimbatore*. Geneva: International Institute for Labour Studies, Discussion Paper Series No. 15.

International Labour Office 1971. *Matching Employment Opportunities and Expectations*. Geneva: International Labour Office.

International Labour Office 1972. *Employment, Incomes and Equality: A Strategy for Increasing Productive Employment in Kenya*. Geneva: International Labour Office.

International Labour Office 1974. *Sharing in Development in the Philippines*. Geneva: International Labour Office.

International Labour Office 1981. *First Thing First. Meeting the Basic Needs of the People of Nigeria*. Geneva: International Labour Office.

Jackson, D. 1979. The disappearance of strikes in Tanzania: incomes policy and industrial democracy. *Journal of Modern African Studies* 17, 2, 219–51.

Jecchinis, C. 1978. The role of trade unions in the social development of Greece. In *The Role of Trade Unions in Developing Societies*, E. M. Kassalow & U. G. Damachi (eds). Geneva: International Institute for Labour Studies.

Kannappan, S. 1977. *Studies in Urban Labour Market Behaviour in Developing Areas*. Geneva: International Institute for Labour Studies.

Kassalow, E. M. 1963. *National Labour Movements in the Postwar World*. Evanston, Ill.: Northwestern University Press.

Kassalow, E. M. 1969. *Trade Unions and Industrial Relations: An International Comparison*. New York: Random.

Kassalow, E. M. & U. G. Damachi (eds) 1978. *The Role of Trade Unions in Developing Societies*. Geneva: International Institute for Labour Studies.

Kerr, C. *et al.* 1960. *Industrialism and Industrial Man*. Cambridge, Mass.: Harvard University Press.

Killick, Tony 1973. Price controls in Africa: the Ghana experience. *Journal of Modern African Studies* 11, 3, 405–26.

Kirkpatrick, C. H. & F. I. Nixson 1976. The origins of inflation in less developed countries: a selective review. In *Inflation in Open Economies*, M. Parkin & G. Zis (eds), 126–74. Manchester: Manchester University Press.

Martens, G. R. 1979. Industrial relations in French-speaking West Africa. In *Industrial Relations in Africa*, U. G. Damachi *et al.* (eds). London: Macmillan.

Meynaud, J. & A. Saleh-Bey 1967. *Trade Unionism in Africa*. London: Methuen.

Millen, B. H. 1963. *The Political Role of Labour in Developing Countries*. Washington, DC: Brookings.

Mohammed-Taha, S. A. 1979. Evolution of pay structure in the Sudan: 1948–1978. Unpublished PhD thesis, University of Sussex.

Muir, J. D. & J. L. Brown 1978. The changing role of government in collective bargaining. In *The Role of Trade Unions in Developing Societies*, E. M. Kassalow & U. G. Damachi (eds). Geneva: International Institute for Labour Studies.

Munck, R. 1987. The labour movement in Argentina and Brazil. A comparative perspective. In *International Labour and the Third World*, R. E. Boyd *et al.* (eds). London: Gower.

Ogle, G. 1978. Changing character of labour–government–management relations in the Republic of Korea. In *The Role of Trade Unions in Developing Societies*, E. M. Kassalow & U. G. Damachi (eds). Geneva: International Institute for Labour Studies.

Onitiri, H. M. A. & K. Awosika (eds) 1982. *Inflation in Nigeria*. Ibadan: NISER.

Pang, E. F. & L. Cheng 1978. Changing pattern of industrial relations in Singapore. In *The Role of Trade Unions in Developing Societies*, E. M. Kassalow & U. G. Damachi (eds). Geneva: International Institute for Labour Studies.

Peace, A. 1979. *Choice, Class and Conflict*. Brighton: Harvester.

Pepel, T. J. & K. Tsunekawa 1979. Corporatism without labor: the Japanese anomaly. In *Trends Towards Corporatist Intermediation*, Phillippe C.

Schmitter & Gerhard Lehmbruch (eds), 231–70. Beverly Hills, Calif.: Sage.

Roberts, B. C. 1964. *Labour in the Tropical Territories of the Commonwealth.* London: Bell.

Roberts, B. C. & L. G. de Bellecombe 1967. *Collective Bargaining in African Countries.* New York: St Martins Press.

Routh, G. 1969. Incomes policy in a developing country: a case study of the foreign expert at work (Turner in Tanzania). Department of Economics, University of Dar es Salaam.

Sandbrook, R. 1975. *Proletarians and African Capitalism. The Kenyan Case 1960–72.* Cambridge: Cambridge University Press.

Sandbrook R. & Robin Cohen (eds) 1975. *The Development of an African Working Class.* London: Longman.

Schregle, J. 1982. *Negotiating Development. Labour Relations in Southern Asia.* Geneva: International Labour Office.

Scoville, J. G. 1974. Afghan labour markets: a model of interdependence. *Industrial Relations* **13**, October, 274–87.

Scoville, J. G. 1982. A review of international and comparative research in the 1970s. In *Industrial Relations Research in the 1970s. Review and Appraisal*, T. A. Kochan *et al.* (eds), 1–44. Madison, Wisc.: Industrial Relations Research Association.

Sethuraman, S. V. (ed.) 1981. *The Urban Informal Sector in the Developing Countries.* Geneva: International Labour Office.

Shivji, Isa 1976. *Class Struggles in Tanzania.* London: Heinemann.

Smock, D. R. 1969. *Conflict and Control in an African Trade Union.* Stanford, Calif.: Hoover.

Southall, R. 1987. *Labour and Unions in Asia and Africa. Contemporary Struggles.* London: Macmillan.

Southall, R. 1988. *Trade Unions and the New Industrialization of the Third World.* London: Zed.

Stewart, F. 1979. The tripartite agreements. In *Essays on Employment in Kenya*, D. Ghai & M. Godfrey (eds). Nairobi: Kenya Literature Bureau.

Sturmthal, A. & J. G. Scoville (eds) 1973. *The International Labour Movement in Transition: Essays on Africa, Asia, Europe and South America.* Urbana, Ill.: University of Illinois Press.

Sunkel, O. 1958. Inflation in Chile: an unorthodox approach. *International Economic Papers* **10**, 107–31.

Thorp, R. 1971. Inflation and the financing of economic development. In *Financing Development in Latin America*, K. Griffin (ed.). London: Macmillan.

Ubeku, A. K. 1983. *Industrial Relations in Developing Countries. The Case of Nigeria.* London: Macmillan.

Warren, W. M. 1966. Urban real wages and the Nigerian trade union movement 1939–60. *Economic Development and Cultural Change* **15**, 1, October, 21–36.

Waterman, P. 1976. Third world strikes: an invitation to a discussion. *Development and Change* **7**, 331–44.

9 Industrial relations in Eastern Europe: recent developments and trends

L. HÉTHY

The theoretical concept of industrial relations has been *unknown* (and *mostly unacceptable*) to scientific thinking and ideology in Eastern Europe for four decades; in fact, there is no proper expression for it in the languages of most of the countries concerned. The reason is obvious: this concept involves a relationship (of conflicts, bargaining and co-operation) among employers, employees, their organizations, and the state that has been supposed not to exist in the centrally planned economies. Moreover, industrial relations appear to be closely associated with market, parliamentary democracy, freedom of association, strikes and lock-outs – attributes of industrial market economies that have always been considered as 'alien' to socialism. Nowadays, however, it has to be admitted (and has been admitted in most countries recently or some long time ago as in Hungary and Poland) that conflicts are self-evident even in a 'socialist' economy; employers and employees are autonomous actors in the economy (consequently their organizations have to function on that basis), bargaining is a flexible and efficient tool of conflict-solving; after all, there is a need for an institutionalized industrial relations system – and it has to be (and can only be) worked out within the framework of broader economic and political reforms. Market and political pluralism are given more and more emphasis. In this context, *very topical questions are*: what the until recently 'non-existent' industrial relations system looks like in Eastern Europe, what recent developments and trends can be perceived in the relationship of employers, employees and the state, and what the prospects are for the future.

state + party
representation (power) of working
class, ownership of means of
production

employers = state
bureaucrats (co-owners)
taking care of means of
production

trade unions
'transmission belt'
from state + party
to working class
(employers + employees)

employees
working class
(co-owners) of means of
production

Figure 9.1   The traditional Stalinist industrial relations model

The traditional Stalinist model

In industrial relations Stalinist monolithic patterns (Figure 9.1) *have
dominated in most Eastern European countries up to now*. In
this traditional concept of industrial relations, the state (party and
government), employers (enterprises) and trade unions (employees'
organizations) are supposed to act in 'full harmony' on the basis
of the ideology of 'one prevailing social interest' (originating from
the socialist – predominantly state – ownership of property). This
general interest is supposed to unite everyone in the 'construction
of socialism': partners in industrial relations are instructed by the
infallible and omnipotent Communist Party, the 'incarnation' of
the dictatorship by the working class. In a highly centralized
decision-making process, excluding real social consultation and
relying on the scientific foundations of Marxism, the state works
out the 'one best way' for joint social action in the framework of
a bureaucratic central planning system and closely supervises the
realization of the targets set by similarly rigid bureaucratic control.
In this model, introduced in the period of rapid industrialization
and collectivization in agriculture (in the Soviet Union at the end of
the 1920s, in the rest of Eastern Europe in the early 1950s), neither
employers nor trade unions can be identified as autonomous actors

in industrial relations; the former are state bureaucrats taking care of state property on the basis of rigid and detailed bureaucratic instructions; the latter have the role of 'transmission belt', i.e. they hand down central will and decisions to workers. In general, the state, the employers and the trade unions constitute one monolithic centre of power – predominated by the state – with no distinct separate functions. In this Stalinist model, collective labour disputes and conflicts of interests are looked upon as non-existent (strikes, as actions of workers against their own interests, are superfluous). If divergences of interests and conflicts appear, they are interpreted as manifestations of individual misbehaviour, violations of the law or 'socialist morality' and treated accordingly. Labour law is often applied as a means of disciplining deviant individuals. Although until recently prevailing in most of Eastern Europe (the Soviet Union, Romania, Czechoslovakia, and East Germany), this traditional model of industrial relations has been repeatedly put into question by situations of economic and political crisis (Hungary 1956, Czechoslovakia 1968, Poland early 1980s). Present economic difficulties, social unrest and political tensions – and recently the collapse of the past monolithic political systems – however, have entailed a challenge to the model which earlier could not have been foreseen.

Signs of progress

Under the pressure of their well-known historical, economic, social, and political problems, Hungary and Poland were the first to start *a cautious revision of the Stalinist ideological and institutional foundations*, although for the moment it would be too early to declare that a new model of industrial relations has been born.

(1)   A milestone in this process was Hungary's economic reform in 1968 (followed at first cautiously and then more vigorously by several other countries at the end of the 1980s; examples are the Soviet Law on Enterprises, 1987 and the economic reform launched by Czechoslovakia's past communist regime), which increased the role of market, recognized enterprises as autonomous centres of decision-making, restored profitability as the main indicator of economic success, emphasized the primary importance of material incentives, and loosened up the

direct and detailed control of state agencies (and of the central plan) over the economy. Hungary made several further steps towards 'deregulation', 'liberalization', 'de-bureaucratization' – offering a relatively wide scope for the private sector as well. Needless to say, such measures do not fit into the Stalinist pattern of industrial relations.

(2) In its ideology, the ruling Hungarian Communist Party (HSWP) recognized already in the 1970s the 'objective' existence of diverging and conflicting interests – among others those of the workers (employees), of the enterprises (employers) and of the state agencies – and called for their institutionalization as well as for a distinct separation of the respective role of trade unions, employers and the state.

(3) The Hungarian trade unions gave up their traditional 'transmission belt' function as early as the end of the 1960s. For 20 years they set themselves a 'double function' (both to promote production and to represent workers' interests) and it was declared in 1988 that in the future they would limit themselves to the representation of workers' interests.

In 1975–80 trade union rights (concerning all issues of working and living conditions) were considerably extended and enterprise-level trade union organization reformed, i.e. it was put under closer control by its members. At the same time, trade unions gave up their state functions (the control of social security and occupational safety systems). In 1988–9 new independent trade unions emerged (united by the Democratic League of Independent Trade Unions) although their membership is mostly white-collar and not yet significant.

(4) Employers (enterprises) have become more and more important autonomous actors in the industrial relations scene during the past 20 years. Their organization, the Hungarian Chamber of Economy (which had 700 member enterprises in 1984 and 1500 in 1988), earlier limited itself to the promotion of foreign trade, relations between its members, etc. Nowadays it is a more or less influential actor in central decision-making, representing the interests of Hungarian employers.

(5) New institutions have been established to prevent and to solve collective labour disputes over rights and interests (including a double structure of enterprise-level participation, the right of veto of trade unions to suspend employers' measures considered as injurious, regular consultations between

the government and the National Council of Trade Unions which has been transformed into an institution of tripartite concertation (National Council for the Conciliation of Interests, 1988), and a law on strikes).

Hungary's cautious progress in the reform of its industrial relations system (lagging somewhat behind the turbulent developments in Poland in the early 1980s) constituted by no means as yet a radical shift away from its Stalinist foundations. It was impeded by a slowdown in economic reform in the 1970s and in particular by the postponement of the reform of the political system. Still, Hungary at the end of the 1980s appeared to be far ahead of most of Eastern Europe in this field.

Participation and collective bargaining

Participation, if properly applied, can be a major instrument to prevent labour disputes and conflicts and to maintain co-operation between employer and employee. In Eastern Europe a host of institutions of *direct* and *indirect* (via workers' representatives) forms of participation have been developed over the past 40 years. To participation, in accordance with the essential philosophies concerning industrial relations, is attributed *four major* (openly declared or tacitly followed) *functions*:

(a) *legitimation of the political system*: it has always been a strong argument in favour of the socialist political system (in compensation for the well-known weaknesses of parliamentary democracy) that 'enterprises are run by the workers' collectives themselves';

(b) *promotion of economic performance*: in some countries (East Germany, Soviet Union), participation has been looked upon as a 'direct productive force' channelling workers' innovations to the production process;

(c) *conflict-solving*: to prevent individual and collective labour disputes of rights and interests (as it has been considered in Hungary and Poland) for the past decade;

(d) *the realization of social values* (such as collectivism and the development of 'socialist personality', whatever the latter means).

In Eastern Europe, varying from country to country and over time (even within a given country), the above functions of participation have been given differing emphasis – some have been overemphasized and others neglected.

As for the institutions of enterprise-level participation, three models can be identified although the dividing lines between them are very often far from being distinct:

(a) first, *participation via trade unions* – a model that has existed in Czechoslovakia and East Germany (probably because of the strong industrial and trade union traditions of these countries) for some time;

(b) secondly, *self-management type participation* – in Bulgaria, Poland and Romania – where workers have had the right to participate in decision-making via institutions that have been related or unrelated to trade union activities (workers' assemblies and their executive bodies called workers' councils, enterprise councils, etc.);

(c) thirdly, *mixed type of participation* (in Hungary and the Soviet Union).

Hungary's mixed-type double structure of enterprise-level participation is a good example of participation aimed at the prevention and solution of conflicts and at the promotion of economic performance.

On the one hand, *shop stewards* (direct representatives of trade union membership) *and their committees* have had a right of co-decision on a number of issues concerning the living and working conditions of workers (such as the conclusion and control of the implementation of collective agreements, enterprise wage policies, setting up of incentive schemes, setting individual wages, etc.) and they have had to be consulted on a number of issues related to the functioning of the enterprise (production planning, organizational changes, etc.). Shop stewards were promoted to their key position in the period between 1975 and 1980.

On the other hand, *enterprise councils*, made up of management's and workers' representatives (independent of trade union and party) in equal numbers, were set up in the period 1984–6 and have had the right of decision on all major economic issues (production planning, investments, marketing, price policies, etc.) concerning the functioning of the enterprise and giving the employer rights over the enterprise's director, including his or her election and dismissal. (In small enterprises, workers' assemblies have these functions.)

This double structure of participation in Hungary (although an outcome of the play of conflicting concepts and political intentions) *has contributed to*

(a) the prevention and solution of collective labour disputes over rights and interests;
(b) a separation of employers' and trade union roles;
(c) a revision of the anachronistic concept in socialist law of 'one-man responsibility' for the functioning of the enterprise;
(d) an increased autonomy of enterprises towards state agencies.

Participation, however, as referred to earlier, has had a very *different meaning and significance* in Eastern Europe: while in some countries its institutions have a real role in conflict-solving, in others they are limited to the promotion of production or to a ritual approval and implementation of central political will. In Romania, for example, workers' councils – at first sight very similar institutions to the Hungarian enterprise councils – on closer examination were found to be mere reproductions of traditional enterprise leadership (uniting top management, top trade union and party functionaries) and limited to carrying out the rigid and detailed instructions of state agencies, the enterprises having practically no autonomy in the given economic guidance system.

Participation is usually closely related to *collective bargaining*. The latter is often looked upon as a fundamental form of participation in literature.

Eastern Europe *has collective contracts* in the industrial relations field (most countries have had both branch- and enterprise-level collective contracts, while Hungary only enterprise-level contracts), but it has had *no* (or very limited) *collective bargaining* in the original market economy sense of the word. Without entering into a discussion of the extremely complicated legal framework of collective agreements, I would like to underline some of their general features.

(a) *The lack of real bargaining* has been self-evident in the traditional model of industrial relations. Where no conflicts of collective interests are supposed to exist (and this is an

Table 9.1 Socialist collective agreements.

Country	Sector			Enterprise	
	Including rights and duties following from labour relations (normative)	With supervisory or directive character	With the undertaking of obligations	Including rights and duties following from labour relations (normative)	With the undertaking of obligations
Bulgaria	–	–	–	–	×
Czechoslovakia	×	×	×	×	×
Germany, East	×	–	–	×	×
Hungary	–	–	–	×	–
Poland	×	×	–	–	–
Romania	–	×	–	×	×
Soviet Union	–	×	–	×	×

Source: L. Nagy, *The socialist collective agreement*, Budapest: Akadémiai Kiadó, 1984, p. 39.

essential assumption in this model) there is no need or room for collective bargaining.

(b)   Collective contracts often have had in many countries (excluding Hungary and Poland) *a supervisory character*, formulating obligations by the supervisory state organs for the 'workers' collectives'. In Hungary they are limited to formulating rights and duties of employers and employees arising from the employment relationship.

(c)   Collective agreements have often *included disciplinary measures* by the 'workers' collective' to sanction the behaviour of deviant members.

(d)   As for the rights and duties arising from the employment relationship, they have very often been *mere repetitions of* the detailed regulations of *labour law* (a practice that is somewhat justified by over-regulation, preventing both employers and employees from finding their way through the 'jungle' of valid regulations). Where enterprise autonomy has started to develop (as in Hungary), collective agreements, however, contain an increasing set of issues settled at enterprise level (such as incentive schemes, performance standard setting, etc.).

(e)   In many cases even *the definite contents* of collective contracts have been *prescribed by law* and there has been no legal room to include additional issues (a limit that has been abolished, for example, in Hungary).

To sum up, while in the market economy countries the major function of collective bargaining appears to be to settle issues between employers and employees beyond the standards set by the state and in fields not regulated by the state, in the socialist countries collective agreements have been mostly limited to the local 'operationalization' (or a mere repetition) of central instructions. That is why their essence – to prevent conflicts and maintain co-operation by an institutionalized bargaining process between parties of diverging and conflicting interests – has been mostly missing.

The settlement of labour disputes

In Eastern Europe *there has been no statutory procedure* (except in Poland and in a sense in Hungary) *for the settlement of collective labour disputes* over rights and interests: if such conflicts occurred they were smoothed over by informal, i.e. non-institutionalized, interventions by state, party and trade union organs. 'In Eastern Europe we spend more time and energy on concealing conflicts than on solving them', a Hungarian sociologist commented in the 1970s. Despite this general picture, certain signs of progress have appeared.

First, a specific *Hungarian* invention in this field is the *trade union's right of veto* (going back to the 1970s) which can be applied both in cases of collective and individual labour disputes, suspending the employer's measure considered as being injurious and subjecting it to revision by higher trade union and state organs. This right of veto has proved to be a successful weapon (in 80 to 90 per cent of the cases the employer's measures have been revised), but it has been applied with great caution (200 to 300 annual applications) and Hungarian trade unions, as admitted even by their top leadership, have shied away too often from its application. In the Soviet Union, according to recent trade union declarations, the introduction of a similar legal institution is under consideration.

Secondly, the *Polish Law on Strikes*, 1982 (prepared at that time with the participation of Solidarity) established definite institutions for conciliation and arbitration of collective labour disputes and regulated strikes, while prohibiting political strikes. A similar law was enacted in Hungary in March 1989, followed by a Strike Act in the Soviet Union.

This touches upon the most sensitive issue of industrial relations in Eastern Europe. While *strikes* have occurred frequently (in Poland) or occasionally (in most socialist countries: Hungary, Bulgaria, Romania, the Soviet Union), to speak about them as an inevitable part of industrial relations was equal to blasphemy in most of these countries. Hungary's attitude towards them has been rather awkward too. While Hungarian law has never prohibited strikes (in fact in 1976 Hungary joined an international convention that contained the right to strike), nothing was done about their legal regulation for the following 12 years. The pros and cons were reasoned as follows:

(a) Strikes cause severe damage to the economy;
(b) They undermine social co-operation and political stability;
(c) The rare and sporadic strikes Hungary had could be settled by the traditional (informal) interventions of state, party and trade union organs;

(d) Strikes question the traditional image of 'socialism' as a society free of conflicts;

(e) As there is a lack of institutions for the settlement of collective labour disputes, strikes tend to end up as a series of individual labour disputes over rights (cases of disciplinary liability); they may remain unsettled and can generate political tensions.

While nobody feels happy about the possibility of having more strikes, for us it appears obvious that Hungary (and the rest of the socialist countries) has been badly in need of statutory procedures to settle collective labour conflicts over rights and interests – as such conflicts exist – and such statutory procedures probably could not exclude the right to strike as the ultimate weapon of the workers.

For decades most Eastern European countries had only legal *institutions for the settlement of individual labour disputes over rights*. These institutions differ in their structure, procedures and function, with varying levels of success. In Hungary, for example, such disputes are dealt with in the first instance by so-called Labour Arbitration Committees at the enterprise level (social bodies that are supposed to be independent of both employer and trade union); in the second instance by special labour courts whose activities are supervised by the Labour Law Chamber of the Supreme Court. This institutional machinery, although it has probably contributed to the settlement of a large number of labour disputes, has demonstrated *definite weaknesses*:

(a) While tensions in industrial relations have kept growing, the number of cases dealt with by Hungarian Labour Arbitration Committees has declined from 50 000 in 1980 to 34 000 in 1986;

(b) A large number of Labour Arbitration Committees have been kept idle: more than half of them have had only one or two cases, or none at all, submitted to them annually;

(c) The majority of labour disputes have been over material liability, disciplinary liability and liability for custody cases; thus, important issues (concerning remuneration, employment, etc.) have mostly not been dealt with by these institutions.

In general, these institutions for the settlement of individual labour disputes over rights – by their nature and the political and socioeconomic context of their functioning – have always been inappropriate for treating major industrial conflicts.

Formalism (i.e. functioning according to the rules without real content) has been an essential general weakness of the institutions of industrial relations functioning in the traditional Stalinist system. If industrial relations are looked upon as monolithic participation, it follows that collective bargaining and labour dispute settlement degenerate to a merely formal procedure without any realistic content: meetings are held, participants voice their opinions, contributions are registered in minutes and no further action is taken.

Wage determination: an example

In the context of the present possibilities and limits of industrial relations in Eastern Europe, the best example of its functioning is offered by wage determination.

Wage determination in all of the socialist countries has been basically a bureaucratic process in which the state has had a predominant influence: it is the state which basically determines wages by its powerful means (by its direct instructions or indirect regulations based on the plan, by setting up obligatory central job-evaluation systems and wage scales, even by centrally describing performance standards). It controls the wage level and major wage structures of the national economy, the wage fund (wage level) of enterprises, as well as very often even individual basic wages. This process has had very little to do with the labour market – the existence of which has been mostly ignored or denied – or with the essential needs of the major parties in industrial relations – those of employers and employees. On the contrary, it has always been subordinated entirely to the targets of general economic policy and to abstract ideological considerations. In Eastern Europe, industrialization – and, in recent times, the budget balance and the balance of payments in some countries – has been primarily financed by keeping consumption (and most of all wages) at a depressed level. As a result, the functioning of national wage systems has gradually arrived at a state of crisis.

(a) Wages (together with social benefits) very often barely cover the cost of living.

(b) Enterprises cannot attract and motivate labour. Wages are a special (somewhat scarce) 'labelled' item in the structure of their costs that is a source of economically irrational decisions.

(c) Wage structures are distorted. Non-manual (intellectual) work and non-material activities are undervalued by the wage system.

(d) Wage differentials in general are levelled off (e.g. those of manual and non-manual workers, of the material and non-material sphere) but they can be considerable in identical jobs.

(e) The depressed level of wages leads to a general restriction of output (both at enterprise and individual level) and is a source of social and political unrest.

To meet these challenges, the Hungarian and Polish reforms (in the 1970s and the early 1980s), as well as the ones in the Soviet Union, Czechoslovakia and Bulgaria at the end of the 1980s, initiated certain changes in wage determination. On the one hand, intervention by the state took less direct forms (e.g. the 'wage fund' of enterprises, whose increase was linked with certain 'success indicators', such as profits, to 'motivate' the workers' collective); on the other hand, a certain autonomy was introduced for enterprise-level decision-making (in Hungary in the selection of incentive schemes, in setting individual wages, performance standards, etc.). While such developments proved to be beneficial in the short run by loosening up somewhat earlier rigid practices, they left, however, the predominating role of the state in wage determination untouched. That is why now in Hungary the 'indirect' or 'decentralized' forms of wage determination by the state described above are looked upon as a failure (although they are still greatly advertised in the Soviet Union) and wage reform has been put on the agenda once again. Hungary has arrived at the conclusion that the only way to achieve a sound wage system, i.e. rational and equitable wages, is offered by the mechanism of the market economies: to base wage determination on the labour market on the one hand and on collective bargaining on the other hand. The first steps in this direction were already made in 1988.

Progress in this direction, however, is burdened by immense difficulties:

(a) There is powerful pressure both by trade unions and employers to increase wages (risking even more rapid inflation).

(b) There are no institutional guarantees that either employers' organizations or trade unions can represent effectively the interests of their membership.

(c) There are as yet no sufficient statutory procedures (conciliation, arbitration) to settle collective labour disputes.

(d) The state is hesitant to loosen its grip on wage determination in a situation of economic crisis (international debts, failing economic performance, high inflation), although its practices do not seem to be compatible with reform measures in other fields aimed at the promotion of entrepreneurship and the role of the market.

(e) The present grave distortions of the wage system, a heritage of the past 40 years, probably cannot be healed without certain direct interventions by the state.

In 1989 Hungary arrived at a breakthrough: a new (hitherto in Eastern Europe the most liberal) wage determination system was introduced. In it enterprises are free to adopt their wage level and structures to their own strategies and the labour market – increases in the wage fund are burdened by relatively moderate taxes of which small undertakings and joint ventures are exempt – and a tripartite body – the National Council for the Conciliation of Interests – is to formulate and implement national wage policies. It takes decisions as to guaranteed minimum wages, adopts recommendations as to minimum and maximum wage increases by the enterprises, etc. Although this system has been much criticized, it has not speeded up inflation and is a definite step towards a market economy model of wage determination.

Towards the market economy model

While in 1988–9 it was hard to identify clear trends in industrial relations – beyond positive signs primarily in Hungary and Poland – we are in a better position to do so now. Most of Eastern Europe opted for pluralistic parliamentary democracy – Hungary and Poland in a 'peaceful transition', Czechoslovakia and East Germany by toppling their past hardline Communist regimes; and political changes are going on in Bulgaria, Romania and the Soviet

Union as well. At the same time political change has speeded up economic reforms: privatization and marketization is gaining impetus: several countries have decided – in a more or less determined way – to move towards a market economy. Even the Soviets appear to have unwillingly become accustomed to this idea. If these political and economic preconditions are given – even if in political programmes or slogans and not so much in existing realities – there is only one way for the development of industrial relations and it is towards the market economy model(s). Trends in the individual countries, often identical, often differing, appear to point in this direction: by the collapse of the past political system the central bureaucratic guidance (and planning) of the national economies is being pulled down; a separation of state, employers' and workers' representative organizations is going on; employers are reinforced by the process of privatization; a pluralization of workers' organizations is taking place in several countries: the traditional trade unions are undergoing considerable internal changes and seek for legitimacy while new alternative trade unions appear on the scene (for example, in Hungary and Bulgaria following the example of Polish Solidarity) and – at a much slower speed – a development of up-to-date institutions of industrial relations is starting.

state =
representation of public
interests, public
administration, owner of
majority of means of
production

party =
political
organization

employers' organization =
representation of employers'
(enterprises') interests

trade unions =
representation of employees'
(workers) interests

employers =
managers of state (and
private) enterprises

employees' =
hired workers
(wage earners)

Figure 9.2 The new alternative industrial relations model

Further progress in industrial relations, in principle, will be determined by the existing social partners; in practice, primarily by the political will once again: this time by the attitudes of the new legitimate governments and legislators. These appear to be influenced however by past (realized or missing) developments, the existence (or lack) of historical traditions, the pressure of topical tasks – of how to manage the economic crisis and inevitable restructuring and minimize social tensions and conflicts – and the (closer or looser) relationship with the 'model' Western industrialized market economies. Eastern Europe has a lot to learn from them but it probably cannot find ready-made solutions for its own problems: it has to 'sweat out' its own way.

Index